Ninja Dual Zone Air Fryer

Cookbook for Beginners

Nutritious and Cutting-edge Ninja Air Fryer Recipes Designed for Busy Home Cooks, with Twice the Flavor and Half the Time

Molly Schofield

CONTENTS

INTRODUCTION 6

What is the Ninja Dual Zone Air Fryer? 7
How does Ninja Dual Zone Air Fryer work? 7
How Ninja Dual Zone Air Fryer is different from traditional air fryer? 8
How to clean and maintain the Ninja Dual Zone Air Fryer? 10

MEASUREMENT CONVERSIONS 11

SNACKS AND APPETIZERS RECIPES 13

Potato Tater Tots 14
Cheese Corn Fritters 14
Chili-lime Crispy Chickpeas Pizza-seasoned Crispy Chickpeas 14
Dried Apple Chips Dried Banana Chips 15
Crispy Tortilla Chips 15
Jalapeño Popper Dip With Tortilla Chips 15
Parmesan Crush Chicken 16
Healthy Spinach Balls 16
Dijon Cheese Sandwich 17
Spicy Chicken Tenders 17
Kale Potato Nuggets 17
Cauliflower Cheese Patties 17
Avocado Fries With Sriracha Dip 18
Potato Chips 18
Tasty Sweet Potato Wedges 18
Chicken Stuffed Mushrooms 19
Miso-glazed Shishito Peppers Charred Lemon Shishito Peppers 19
Crab Cake Poppers 19
Mexican Jalapeno Poppers 20
Mac And Cheese Balls 20
Crispy Popcorn Shrimp 20
Cheddar Quiche 21
Garlic Bread 21
Tofu Veggie Meatballs 21
Beef Jerky Pineapple Jerky 21
Chicken Tenders 22
Stuffed Bell Peppers 22
Grill Cheese Sandwich 22

BREAKFAST RECIPES 23
Strawberry Baked Oats Chocolate Peanut Butter Baked Oats 24
Brussels Sprouts Potato Hash 24
Breakfast Sausage Omelet 25
Bacon And Egg Omelet 25
Breakfast Cheese Sandwich 25
Blueberry Coffee Cake And Maple Sausage Patties 26
Morning Egg Rolls 26
Sweet Potato Sausage Hash 27
Egg And Avocado In The Ninja Foodi 27
Cornbread 27
Pumpkin French Toast Casserole With Sweet And Spicy Twisted Bacon 28
Egg White Muffins 28
Lemon-cream Cheese Danishes Cherry Danishes 29
Breakfast Bacon 29
Easy Pancake Doughnuts 29
Egg With Baby Spinach 30
Yellow Potatoes With Eggs 30
Healthy Oatmeal Muffins 30
Banana And Raisins Muffins 31
Sweet Potato Hash 31
Pepper Egg Cups 31
Air Fryer Sausage Patties 31
Honey Banana Oatmeal 32
Hash Browns 32
Donuts 32
Bagels 32
Breakfast Stuffed Peppers 33
Cinnamon-raisin Bagels Everything Bagels 33

POULTRY RECIPES 34
Balsamic Duck Breast 35
Crispy Fried Quail 35
Chicken And Broccoli 36
Thai Chicken Meatballs 36
Honey Butter Chicken 37
Cheddar-stuffed Chicken 37
Chicken Breast Strips 37
Turkey Burger Patties 37
Chicken Drumsticks 38
Lemon Chicken Thighs 38
“fried” Chicken With Warm Baked Potato Salad 38
Chicken Vegetable Skewers 39
Chicken Wings 39
Italian Chicken & Potatoes 39
Spicy Chicken Wings 40
Cornish Hen With Asparagus 40
Teriyaki Chicken Skewers 40

Chicken Potatoes....41
Chicken Parmesan With Roasted Lemon-parmesan Broccoli....41
Jamaican Fried Chicken....42
Dijon Chicken Wings....42
Chicken Caprese....43
Asian Chicken....43
Chicken Parmesan....43
Air-fried Turkey Breast With Roasted Green Bean Casserole....44
Chili Chicken Wings....44
Chicken Fajitas With Street Corn....45
Thai Curry Chicken Kabobs....45

BEEF, PORK, AND LAMB RECIPES....46

Steak And Mashed Creamy Potatoes....47
Beef Kofta Kebab....47
Cheesesteak Taquitos....47
Barbecue Ribs With Roasted Green Beans And Shallots....48
Steak In Air Fry....48
Chinese Bbq Pork....48
Balsamic Steak Tips With Roasted Asparagus And Mushroom Medley....49
Korean Bbq Beef....49
Curry-crusted Lamb Chops With Baked Brown Sugar Acorn Squash....50
Air Fried Lamb Chops....50
Pork Chops....50
Tomahawk Steak....51
Beef Ribs Ii....51
Tasty Lamb Patties....51
Bacon Wrapped Pork Tenderloin....52
Garlic Butter Steaks....52
Bell Peppers With Sausages....52
Spicy Lamb Chops....52
Lamb Shank With Mushroom Sauce....53
Steak Bites With Cowboy Butter....53
Zucchini Pork Skewers....54
Sausage Meatballs....54
Easy Breaded Pork Chops....54
Short Ribs & Root Vegetables....55
Parmesan Pork Chops....55
Marinated Pork Chops....55
Cilantro Lime Steak....56
Pork Tenderloin With Brown Sugar–pecan Sweet Potatoes....56

FISH AND SEAFOOD RECIPES....57

Crispy Catfish....58
Honey Teriyaki Tilapia....58
Sesame Honey Salmon....58
Healthy Lobster Cakes....59
Tuna Steaks....59

Herb Tuna Patties 59
Shrimp Po'boys With Sweet Potato Fries 60
Herb Lemon Mussels 60
Lemon Pepper Fish Fillets 61
Fish Sandwich 61
Fish And Chips 61
Salmon With Coconut 62
Roasted Salmon And Parmesan Asparagus 62
Pretzel-crusted Catfish 62
Furikake Salmon 63
Smoked Salmon 63
Scallops 63
Frozen Breaded Fish Fillet 64
Shrimp Skewers 64
Chili Lime Tilapia 64
Pecan-crusted Catfish Nuggets With "fried" Okra 64
Lemon Pepper Salmon With Asparagus 65
Fried Lobster Tails 65
Savory Salmon Fillets 66
Tasty Parmesan Shrimp 66
Keto Baked Salmon With Pesto 66
Tuna Patties 66
Blackened Mahimahi With Honey-roasted Carrots 67

VEGETABLES AND SIDES RECIPES 68

Green Salad With Crispy Fried Goat Cheese And Baked Croutons 69
Balsamic Vegetables 69
Fried Artichoke Hearts 70
Zucchini Cakes 70
Garlic Potato Wedges In Air Fryer 70
Pepper Poppers 71
Hasselback Potatoes 71
Potatoes & Beans 71
Broccoli, Squash, & Pepper 71
Falafel 72
Buffalo Seitan With Crispy Zucchini Noodles 72
Jerk Tofu With Roasted Cabbage 73
Fresh Mix Veggies In Air Fryer 73
Fried Olives 74
Caprese Panini With Zucchini Chips 74
Potato And Parsnip Latkes With Baked Apples 75
Garlic-herb Fried Squash 75
Beets With Orange Gremolata And Goat's Cheese 76
Herb And Lemon Cauliflower 76
Saucy Carrots 76
Kale And Spinach Chips 77
Garlic-rosemary Brussels Sprouts 77
Buffalo Bites 77
Stuffed Tomatoes 77

Satay-style Tempeh With Corn Fritters......78
Balsamic-glazed Tofu With Roasted Butternut Squash......78
Fried Patty Pan Squash......79
Brussels Sprouts......79

DESSERTS RECIPES......80

Cinnamon Sugar Dessert Fries......81
Apple Crisp......81
Honey Lime Pineapple......81
Chocolate Chip Cake......82
Chocolate Cookies......82
Apple Crumble Peach Crumble......82
Jelly Donuts......83
Bread Pudding......83
Biscuit Doughnuts......83
Healthy Semolina Pudding......84
Cinnamon-sugar "churros" With Caramel Sauce......84
Lemon Sugar Cookie Bars Monster Sugar Cookie Bars......84
Zesty Cranberry Scones......85
Walnuts Fritters......85
Apple Fritters......86
Oreo Rolls......86
Pumpkin Hand Pies Blueberry Hand Pies......87
Baked Apples......87
Lava Cake......87
Moist Chocolate Espresso Muffins......88
Churros......88
Pumpkin Muffins With Cinnamon......89
Dehydrated Peaches......89
Mini Strawberry And Cream Pies......89
Fried Dough With Roasted Strawberries......90
Apple Hand Pies......90
Mini Blueberry Pies......91
Victoria Sponge Cake......91

APPENDIX : RECIPES INDEX......92

INTRODUCTION

My name is Molly Schofield, a professional chef and passionate foodie with years of experience in creating healthy and delicious meals. As someone who understands the importance of good nutrition and healthy eating, I wrote this cookbook to help people make the most of their Ninja Dual Zone Air Fryer and create meals that are both healthy and delicious.

The Ninja Dual Zone Air Fryer Cookbook for Beginners is a comprehensive guide to cooking healthy and delicious meals with your air fryer. Inside this cookbook, you'll find over 100 recipes that are specifically designed for the Ninja Dual Zone Air Fryer, allowing you to make the most of its unique features and capabilities. From crispy chicken wings and roasted vegetables to sweet potato fries and homemade granola, there's something for everyone in this book. Each recipe is carefully crafted to provide maximum flavor and nutrition, while also being easy to prepare and cook.

As a professional chef and nutritionist, I understand the importance of creating meals that are both healthy and delicious. That's why this cookbook is more than just a collection of recipes - it's also a guide to using your Ninja Dual Zone Air Fryer to its full potential. You'll learn about the various cooking functions and settings, as well as tips and tricks for achieving the perfect texture and flavor in your meals. You'll also discover the health benefits of using an air fryer, and how it can help you reduce your intake of unhealthy fats and oils.

The Ninja Dual Zone Air Fryer Cookbook for Beginners is perfect for anyone who wants to create delicious and healthy meals with their air fryer. Whether you're a beginner cook or an experienced chef, this cookbook is the perfect resource for anyone looking to create delicious and healthy meals. With easy-to-follow instructions and mouth-watering photos, this cookbook is perfect for busy people who want to eat healthy without sacrificing flavor or convenience.

The Ninja Dual Zone Air Fryer Cookbook for Beginners is a must-have for anyone who wants to make the most of their air fryer and create delicious and healthy meals. With easy-to-follow recipes, you'll be able to create meals that are both nutritious and delicious, helping you to improve your health and well-being. So why wait? Start cooking healthier and tastier meals today with the Ninja Dual Zone Air Fryer Cookbook for Beginners.

What is the Ninja Dual Zone Air Fryer?

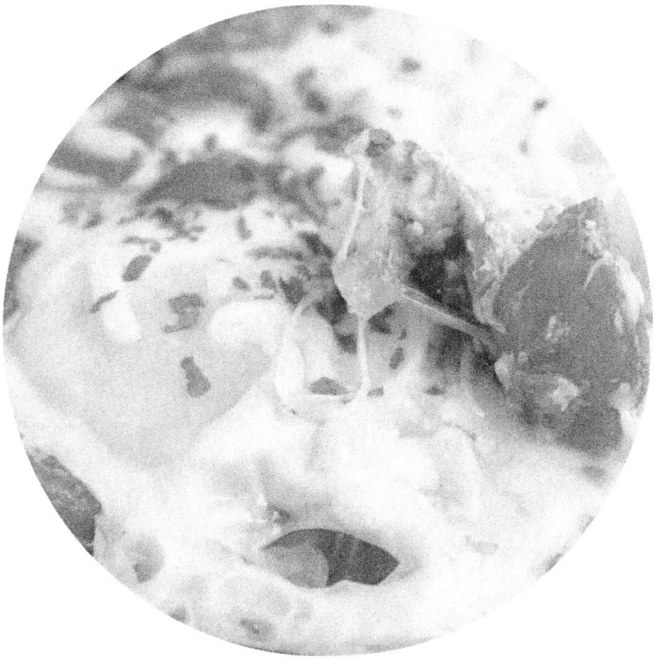

The Ninja Dual Zone Air Fryer is a kitchen appliance that allows users to cook a variety of foods with little to no oil. The device features two independent cooking zones, each with its own temperature and time settings, allowing users to cook two different foods at once.

The Ninja Dual Zone Air Fryer uses air fry technology to cook foods evenly and quickly, resulting in crispy and delicious results every time. The device includes a variety of preset cooking functions, a user-friendly control panel, and a digital timer and temperature control.

It is also designed to be easy to clean, with a non-stick coating on the cooking surfaces and a removable crisper plate. The Ninja Dual Zone Air Fryer is a versatile and convenient appliance that can be used to cook a variety of foods, including meats, vegetables, and desserts, making it a great investment for anyone who wants to cook healthy and delicious meals at home.

How does Ninja Dual Zone Air Fryer work?

Air fry technology is a cooking method that uses hot air to cook foods, producing a crispy and delicious exterior while keeping the interior moist and tender. The Ninja Dual Zone Air Fryer has two independent cooking zones, each with its own temperature and time settings, allowing users to cook two different foods at once.

When using the air fryer, users need to preheat the device to the desired temperature. Once the device is preheated, the cooking basket can be filled with the food to be cooked. The device includes a removable crisper plate, which is designed to help air circulate around the food, ensuring even cooking and a crispy exterior.

Users can select from a variety of preset cooking functions, including air fry, roast, reheat, dehydrate, and bake. Each function is tailored to the specific needs of the food being cooked, ensuring that it is cooked to perfection. The device also includes a digital timer and temperature control, allowing users to adjust the cooking time and temperature to suit their specific needs.

The Ninja Dual Zone Air Fryer is designed to be easy-to-use, with a user-friendly control panel that includes a variety of preset cooking functions. The device also features a cool-touch exterior, ensuring that users don't accidentally burn themselves. The safety feature prevents the basket from being removed during cooking, ensuring that users don't accidentally come into contact with hot surfaces or oil.

After cooking, the device is easy to clean. The cooking basket and crisper plate are removable and dishwasher safe, and the device features a non-stick coating on the cooking surfaces, preventing food from sticking and making it easy to clean.

The Ninja Dual Zone Air Fryer is a versatile and convenient appliance that can be used to cook a variety of foods, including meats, vegetables, and desserts. Its dual zone technology, air fry technology, user-friendly controls, versatility, easy-to-clean design, size and capacity, and safety features make it a great investment for anyone who wants to cook healthy and delicious meals at home. By following the instructions and safety guidelines, users can enjoy crispy and delicious results every time, without the guilt of excess oil and fat.

How Ninja Dual Zone Air Fryer is different from traditional air fryer?

- **Dual Zone Technology**

One of the most significant differences between the Ninja Dual Zone Air Fryer and traditional air fryers is the dual zone technology. The Ninja Dual Zone Air Fryer features two independent cooking zones, each with its own temperature and time settings, allowing users to cook two different foods at once. This means that users can cook a main dish and a side dish at the same time, without having to worry about flavors or aromas mixing. The device also allows users to cook different foods at different temperatures and times, ensuring that each food is cooked to perfection.

- **Large Capacity**

Another difference between the Ninja Dual Zone Air Fryer and traditional air fryers is the size and capacity. The Ninja Dual Zone Air Fryer has a large capacity, allowing users to cook up to 4 quarts of food at once. This is enough to feed a family of four. Traditional air fryers typically have a smaller capacity, making them less suitable for families or larger households.

- **Preset Cooking Functions**

The Ninja Dual Zone Air Fryer includes a variety of preset cooking functions, including air fry, roast, reheat, dehydrate, and bake. These functions are designed to simplify the cooking process and ensure that users get the best results every time. Each function is tailored to the specific needs of the food being cooked, ensuring that it is cooked to perfection. Traditional air fryers may not include as many preset cooking functions, making it more difficult for users to cook a variety of foods.

- **User-Friendly Controls**

The Ninja Dual Zone Air Fryer is designed to be easy-to-use, with a user-friendly control panel that includes a variety of preset cooking functions. The device also features a digital timer and temperature control, allowing users to adjust the cooking time and temperature to suit their specific needs. Traditional air fryers may not include as many user-friendly controls, making them more difficult to use for some users.

- **Crisper Plate**

The Ninja Dual Zone Air Fryer includes a removable crisper plate that is designed to help air circulate around the food. This ensures that the food is cooked evenly and with a crispy exterior. The crisper plate is also designed to be easy to clean, with a non-stick coating that prevents food from sticking to the surface. Traditional air fryers may not include a crisper plate, or it may be more difficult to clean.

- **Safety Features**

The Ninja Dual Zone Air Fryer includes several safety features, including an automatic shut-off function and a cool-touch exterior. The device also includes a safety feature that prevents the basket from being removed during cooking, ensuring that users don't accidentally burn themselves. Traditional air fryers may not include as many safety features, which can be a concern for some users.

How to clean and maintain the Ninja Dual Zone Air Fryer?

- **Unplug the device before cleaning**

Before cleaning the Ninja Dual Zone Air Fryer, it is essential to unplug the device and let it cool down for at least 30 minutes. This will prevent any accidental burns and ensure that the device is safe to handle.

- **Clean the exterior**

To clean the exterior of the Ninja Dual Zone Air Fryer, use a soft, damp cloth to wipe down the surface. Avoid using abrasive or harsh chemicals, as these can damage the surface of the device. If there are any stubborn stains or marks, use a small amount of mild dish soap and warm water to clean the area.

- **Clean the interior**

To clean the interior of the Ninja Dual Zone Air Fryer, first, remove the cooking basket and crisper plate. These can be washed in the dishwasher or by hand with warm, soapy water. Be sure to dry these components thoroughly before replacing them in the device.

Next, use a soft, damp cloth to wipe down the interior of the device. If there are any stubborn stains or marks, use a small amount of mild dish soap and warm water to clean the area. Be sure to avoid getting any water or cleaning solution on the heating element, as this can damage the device.

- **Clean the heating element**

To clean the heating element of the Ninja Dual Zone Air Fryer, first, unplug the device and let it cool down completely. Then, use a soft, damp cloth to wipe down the element. Be sure to avoid using any abrasive or harsh chemicals, as these can damage the element.

- **Clean the fan**

To clean the fan of the Ninja Dual Zone Air Fryer, use a soft, dry cloth to wipe down the blades. Be sure to avoid using any water or cleaning solution on the fan, as this can damage the device.

- **Replace the filter**

The Ninja Dual Zone Air Fryer has a removable air filter that should be cleaned or replaced every 20 cooking cycles. To clean the filter, remove it from the device and wash it with warm, soapy water. Rinse the filter thoroughly and let it dry completely before replacing it in the device. If the filter is damaged or worn, it should be replaced with a new one.

- **Store the device properly**

To ensure that the Ninja Dual Zone Air Fryer stays in good working order, it should be stored in a cool, dry place when not in use. Avoid storing the device in a place where it may be exposed to moisture or extreme temperatures.

By following these cleaning and maintenance guidelines, users can keep their Ninja Dual Zone Air Fryer in top condition, ensuring that it lasts for a long time and continues to produce delicious and healthy meals.

Measurement Conversions

BASIC KITCHEN CONVERSIONS & EQUIVALENTS

DRY MEASUREMENTS CONVERSION CHART

3 TEASPOONS = 1 TABLESPOON = 1/16 CUP

6 TEASPOONS = 2 TABLESPOONS = 1/8 CUP

12 TEASPOONS = 4 TABLESPOONS = 1/4 CUP

24 TEASPOONS = 8 TABLESPOONS = 1/2 CUP

36 TEASPOONS = 12 TABLESPOONS = 3/4 CUP

48 TEASPOONS = 16 TABLESPOONS = 1 CUP

METRIC TO US COOKING CONVERSIONS

OVEN TEMPERATURES

120 °C = 250 °F

160 °C = 320 °F

180° C = 350 °F

205 °C = 400 °F

220 °C = 425 °F

LIQUID MEASUREMENTS CONVERSION CHART

8 FLUID OUNCES = 1 CUP = 1/2 PINT = 1/4 QUART

16 FLUID OUNCES = 2 CUPS = 1 PINT = 1/2 QUART

32 FLUID OUNCES = 4 CUPS = 2 PINTS = 1 QUART

= 1/4 GALLON

128 FLUID OUNCES = 16 CUPS = 8 PINTS = 4 QUARTS = 1 GALLON

BAKING IN GRAMS

1 CUP FLOUR = 140 GRAMS

1 CUP SUGAR = 150 GRAMS

1 CUP POWDERED SUGAR = 160 GRAMS

1 CUP HEAVY CREAM = 235 GRAMS

VOLUME

1 MILLILITER = 1/5 TEASPOON

5 ML = 1 TEASPOON

15 ML = 1 TABLESPOON

240 ML = 1 CUP OR 8 FLUID OUNCES

1 LITER = 34 FL. OUNCES

WEIGHT

1 GRAM = .035 OUNCES

100 GRAMS = 3.5 OUNCES

500 GRAMS = 1.1 POUNDS

1 KILOGRAM = 35 OUNCES

US TO METRIC COOKING CONVERSIONS

1/5 TSP = 1 ML

1 TSP = 5 ML

1 TBSP = 15 ML

1 FL OUNCE = 30 ML

1 CUP = 237 ML

1 PINT (2 CUPS) = 473 ML

1 QUART (4 CUPS) = .95 LITER

1 GALLON (16 CUPS) = 3.8 LITERS

1 OZ = 28 GRAMS

1 POUND = 454 GRAMS

BUTTER

1 CUP BUTTER = 2 STICKS = 8 OUNCES = 230 GRAMS = 8 TABLESPOONS

WHAT DOES 1 CUP EQUAL

1 CUP = 8 FLUID OUNCES

1 CUP = 16 TABLESPOONS

1 CUP = 48 TEASPOONS

1 CUP = 1/2 PINT

1 CUP = 1/4 QUART

1 CUP = 1/16 GALLON

1 CUP = 240 ML

BAKING PAN CONVERSIONS

1 CUP ALL-PURPOSE FLOUR = 4.5 OZ

1 CUP ROLLED OATS = 3 OZ 1 LARGE EGG = 1.7 OZ

1 CUP BUTTER = 8 OZ 1 CUP MILK = 8 OZ

1 CUP HEAVY CREAM = 8.4 OZ

1 CUP GRANULATED SUGAR = 7.1 OZ

1 CUP PACKED BROWN SUGAR = 7.75 OZ

1 CUP VEGETABLE OIL = 7.7 OZ

1 CUP UNSIFTED POWDERED SUGAR = 4.4 OZ

BAKING PAN CONVERSIONS

9-INCH ROUND CAKE PAN = 12 CUPS

10-INCH TUBE PAN =16 CUPS

11-INCH BUNDT PAN = 12 CUPS

9-INCH SPRINGFORM PAN = 10 CUPS

9 X 5 INCH LOAF PAN = 8 CUPS

9-INCH SQUARE PAN = 8 CUPS

Snacks And Appetizers Recipes

Potato Tater Tots

Servings: 4 | Cooking Time: 27 Minutes.

Ingredients:

- 2 potatoes, peeled
- ½ teaspoon Cajun seasoning
- Olive oil cooking spray
- Sea salt to taste

Directions:

1. Boil water in a cooking pot and cook potatoes in it for 15 minutes.
2. Drain and leave the potatoes to cool in a bowl.
3. Grate these potatoes and toss them with Cajun seasoning.
4. Make small tater tots out of this mixture.
5. Divide them into the two crisper plates and spray them with cooking oil.
6. Return the crisper plates to the Ninja Foodi Dual Zone Air Fryer.
7. Choose the Air Fry mode for Zone 1 and set the temperature to 375 degrees F and the time to 27 minutes.
8. Select the "MATCH" button to copy the settings for Zone 2.
9. Initiate cooking by pressing the START/STOP button.
10. Flip them once cooked halfway through, and resume cooking.
11. Serve warm

Nutrition Info:

- (Per serving) Calories 185 | Fat 11g |Sodium 355mg | Carbs 21g | Fiber 5.8g | Sugar 3g | Protein 4.7g

Cheese Corn Fritters

Servings: 6 | Cooking Time: 12 Minutes

Ingredients:

- 1 egg
- 164g corn
- 2 green onions, diced
- 45g flour
- 29g breadcrumbs
- 117g cheddar cheese, shredded
- ½ tsp onion powder
- ½ tsp garlic powder
- 15g sour cream
- Pepper
- Salt

Directions:

1. In a large bowl, add all ingredients and mix until well combined.
2. Insert a crisper plate in the Ninja Foodi air fryer baskets.
3. Make patties from the mixture and place them in both baskets.
4. Select zone 1, then select "air fry" mode and set the temperature to 370 degrees F for 12 minutes. Press "match" to match zone 2 settings to zone 1. Press "start/stop" to begin. Turn halfway through.

Nutrition Info:

- (Per serving) Calories 100 | Fat 4.8g |Sodium 135mg | Carbs 10g | Fiber 1.1g | Sugar 1.5g | Protein 5g

Chili-lime Crispy Chickpeas Pizza-seasoned Crispy Chickpeas

Servings:6 | Cooking Time: 20 Minutes

Ingredients:

- FOR THE CHILI-LIME CHICKPEAS
- 1½ cups canned chickpeas, rinsed and drained
- ¼ cup fresh lime juice
- 1 tablespoon olive oil
- 1½ teaspoons chili powder
- ½ teaspoon kosher salt
- FOR THE PIZZA-SEASONED CHICKPEAS
- 1½ cups canned chickpeas, rinsed and drained
- 1 tablespoon olive oil
- 1 tablespoon grated Parmesan cheese
- ½ teaspoon dried basil
- ½ teaspoon dried oregano
- ½ teaspoon kosher salt
- ¼ teaspoon onion powder
- ¼ teaspoon garlic powder
- ¼ teaspoon fennel seeds
- ¼ teaspoon dried thyme
- ¼ teaspoon red pepper flakes (optional)

Directions:

1. To prep the chili-lime chickpeas: In a small bowl, mix the chickpeas, lime juice, olive oil, chili powder, and salt until the chickpeas are well coated.
2. To prep the pizza-seasoned chickpeas: In a small bowl, mix the chickpeas, olive oil, Parmesan, basil, oregano, salt, onion powder, garlic powder, fennel, thyme, and red pepper flakes (if using) until the chickpeas are well coated.

3. To cook the chickpeas: Install a crisper plate in each of the two baskets. Place the chili-lime chickpeas in the Zone 1 basket and insert the basket in the unit. Place the pizza-seasoned chickpeas in the Zone 2 basket and insert the basket in the unit.
4. Select Zone 1, select AIR FRY, set the temperature to 375°F, and set the time to 20 minutes. Select MATCH COOK to match Zone 2 settings to Zone 1.
5. Press START/PAUSE to begin cooking.
6. When both timers read 10 minutes, press START/PAUSE. Remove both baskets and give each basket a shake to redistribute the chickpeas. Reinsert both baskets and press START/PAUSE to resume cooking.
7. When both timers read 5 minutes, press START/PAUSE. Remove both baskets and give each basket a good shake again. Reinsert both baskets and press START/PAUSE to resume cooking.
8. When cooking is complete, the chickpeas will be crisp and golden brown. Serve warm or at room temperature.

Nutrition Info:

- (Per serving) Calories: 145; Total fat: 6.5g; Saturated fat: 0.5g; Carbohydrates: 17g; Fiber: 4.5g; Protein: 5g; Sodium: 348mg

Dried Apple Chips Dried Banana Chips

Servings:6 | Cooking Time: 6 To 10 Hours

Ingredients:

- FOR THE APPLE CHIPS
- ½ teaspoon ground cinnamon
- ¼ teaspoon ground nutmeg
- ⅛ teaspoon ground allspice
- ⅛ teaspoon ground ginger
- 2 Gala apples, cored and cut into ⅛-inch-thick rings
- FOR THE BANANA CHIPS
- 2 firm-ripe bananas, cut into ¼-inch slices

Directions:

1. To prep the apple chips: In a small bowl, mix the cinnamon, nutmeg, allspice, and ginger until combined. Sprinkle the spice mixture over the apple slices.
2. To dehydrate the fruit: Arrange half of the apple slices in a single layer in the Zone 1 basket. It is okay if the edges overlap a bit as they will shrink as they cook. Place a crisper plate on top of the apples. Arrange the remaining apple slices on top of the crisper plate and insert the basket in the unit.
3. Repeat this process with the bananas in the Zone 2 basket and insert the basket in the unit.
4. Select Zone 1, select DEHYDRATE, set the temperature to 135°F, and set the time to 8 hours.
5. Select Zone 2, select DEHYDRATE, set the temperature to 135°F, and set the time to 10 hours. Select SMART FINISH.
6. Press START/PAUSE to begin cooking.
7. When both timers read 2 hours, press START/PAUSE. Remove both baskets and check the fruit for doneness; note that juicier fruit will take longer to dry than fruit that starts out drier. Reinsert the basket and press START/PAUSE to continue cooking if necessary.

Nutrition Info:

- (Per serving) Calories: 67; Total fat: 0g; Saturated fat: 0g; Carbohydrates: 16g; Fiber: 3g; Protein: 0g; Sodium: 1mg

Crispy Tortilla Chips

Servings: 8 | Cooking Time: 13 Minutes.

Ingredients:

- 4 (6-inch) corn tortillas
- 1 tablespoon Avocado Oil
- Sea salt to taste
- Cooking spray

Directions:

1. Spread the corn tortillas on the working surface.
2. Slice them into bite-sized triangles.
3. Toss them with salt and cooking oil.
4. Divide the triangles in the two crisper plates into a single layer.
5. Return the crisper plates to the Ninja Foodi Dual Zone Air Fryer.
6. Choose the Air Fry mode for Zone 1 and set the temperature to 390 degrees F and the time to 13 minutes.
7. Select the "MATCH" button to copy the settings for Zone 2.
8. Initiate cooking by pressing the START/STOP button.
9. Toss the chips once cooked halfway through, then resume cooking.
10. Serve and enjoy.

Nutrition Info:

- (Per serving) Calories 103 | Fat 8.4g |Sodium 117mg | Carbs 3.5g | Fiber 0.9g | Sugar 1.5g | Protein 5.1g

Jalapeño Popper Dip With Tortilla Chips

Servings:6 | Cooking Time: 15 Minutes

Ingredients:

- FOR THE DIP
- 8 ounces cream cheese, at room temperature
- ½ cup sour cream
- 1 cup shredded Cheddar cheese
- ¼ cup shredded Parmesan cheese
- ¼ cup roughly chopped pickled jalapeños
- ½ teaspoon kosher salt

- ½ cup panko bread crumbs
- 2 tablespoons olive oil
- ½ teaspoon dried parsley
- FOR THE TORTILLA CHIPS
- 10 corn tortillas
- 2 tablespoons fresh lime juice
- 1 tablespoon olive oil
- ½ teaspoon kosher salt

Directions:

1. To prep the dip: In a medium bowl, mix the cream cheese, sour cream, Cheddar, Parmesan, jalapeños, and salt until smooth.
2. In a small bowl, combine the panko, olive oil, and parsley.
3. Pour the dip into a 14-ounce ramekin and top with the panko mixture.
4. To prep the chips: Brush both sides of each tortilla with lime juice, then with oil. Sprinkle with the salt. Using a sharp knife or a pizza cutter, cut each tortilla into 4 wedges.
5. To cook the dip and chips: Install a crisper plate in each of the two baskets. Place the ramekin of dip in the Zone 1 basket and insert the basket in the unit. Layer the tortillas in the Zone 2 basket and insert the basket in the unit.
6. Select Zone 1, select BAKE, set the temperature to 350°F, and set the time to 15 minutes.
7. Select Zone 2, select AIR FRY, set the temperature to 375°F, and set the time to 5 minutes. Select SMART FINISH.
8. Press START/PAUSE to begin cooking.
9. When the Zone 2 timer reads 3 minutes, press START/PAUSE. Remove the basket from the unit and give the basket a good shake to redistribute the chips. Reinsert the basket and press START/PAUSE to resume cooking.
10. When cooking is complete, the dip will be bubbling and golden brown and the chips will be crispy. Serve warm.

Nutrition Info:

- (Per serving) Calories: 406; Total fat: 31g; Saturated fat: 14g; Carbohydrates: 22g; Fiber: 1g; Protein: 11g; Sodium: 539mg

Parmesan Crush Chicken

Servings:4 | Cooking Time:18

Ingredients:

- 4 chicken breasts
- 1 cup parmesan cheese
- 1 cup bread crumb
- 2 eggs, whisked
- Salt, to taste
- Oil spray, for greasing

Directions:

1. Whisk egg in a large bowl and set aside.
2. Season the chicken breast with salt and then put it in egg wash.
3. Next, dredge it in breadcrumb then parmesan cheese.
4. Line both the basket of the air fryer with parchment paper.
5. Divided the breast pieces between the backsets, and oil spray the breast pieces.
6. Set zone 1 basket to air fry mode at 350 degrees F for 18 minutes.
7. Select the MATCH button for the zone 2 basket.
8. Once it's done, serve.

Nutrition Info:

- (Per serving) Calories574 | Fat25g | Sodium848 mg | Carbs 21.4g | Fiber 1.2g| Sugar 1.8g | Protein 64.4g

Healthy Spinach Balls

Servings: 4 | Cooking Time: 10 Minutes

Ingredients:

- 1 egg
- 29g breadcrumbs
- ½ medium onion, chopped
- 225g spinach, blanched & chopped
- 1 carrot, peel & grated
- 1 tbsp cornflour
- 1 tbsp nutritional yeast
- 1 tsp garlic, minced
- ½ tsp garlic powder
- Pepper
- Salt

Directions:

1. Add spinach and remaining ingredients into the mixing bowl and mix until well combined.
2. Insert a crisper plate in the Ninja Foodi air fryer baskets.
3. Make small balls from the spinach mixture and place them in both baskets.
4. Select zone 1, then select "air fry" mode and set the temperature to 390 degrees F for 10 minutes. Press "match" to match zone 2 settings to zone 1. Press "start/stop" to begin.

Nutrition Info:

- (Per serving) Calories 74 | Fat 1.7g |Sodium 122mg | Carbs 11.1g | Fiber 1.9g | Sugar 2g | Protein 4.2g

Dijon Cheese Sandwich

Servings:2 | Cooking Time:10

Ingredients:

- 4 large slices sourdough, whole grain
- 4 tablespoons of Dijon mustard
- 1-1/2 cup grated sharp cheddar cheese
- 2 teaspoons green onion, chopped the green part
- 2 tablespoons of butter melted

Directions:

1. Brush the melted butter on one side of all the bread slices.
2. Then spread Dijon mustard on other sides of slices.
3. Then top the 2 bread slices with cheddar cheese and top it with green onions.
4. Cover with the remaining two slices to make two sandwiches.
5. Divide it between two baskets of the air fryer.
6. Turn on the air fry mode for zone 1 basket at 350 degrees f, for 10 minutes.
7. Use the match button for the second zone.
8. Once it's done, serve.

Nutrition Info:

- (Per serving) calories 617| fat 38 g| sodium 1213mg | carbs40.8 g | fiber 5g| sugar 5.6g | protein 29.5g

Spicy Chicken Tenders

Servings:2 | Cooking Time:12

Ingredients:

- 2 large eggs, whisked
- 2 tablespoons lemon juice
- Salt and black pepper
- 1 pound of chicken tenders
- 1 cup Panko breadcrumbs
- 1/2 cup Italian bread crumb
- 1 teaspoon smoked paprika
- 1/4 teaspoon garlic powder
- 1/4 teaspoon onion powder
- 1/2 cup fresh grated parmesan cheese

Directions:

1. Take a bowl and whisk eggs in it and set aside for further use.
2. In a large bowl add lemon juice, paprika, salt, black pepper, garlic powder, onion powder
3. In a separate bowl mix Panko breadcrumbs, Italian bread crumbs, and parmesan cheese.
4. Dip the chicken tender in the spice mixture and coat the entire tender well.
5. Let the tenders sit for 1 hour.
6. Then dip each chicken tender in egg and then in bread crumbs.
7. Line both the basket of the air fryer with parchment paper.
8. Divide the tenders between the baskets.
9. Set zone 1 basket to air fry mode at 350 degrees F for 12 minutes.
10. Select the MATCH button for the zone 2 basket.
11. Once it's done, serve.

Nutrition Info:

- (Per serving) Calories 836| Fat 36g| Sodium1307 mg | Carbs 31.3g | Fiber 2.5g| Sugar3.3 g | Protein 95.3g

Kale Potato Nuggets

Servings: 4 | Cooking Time: 15minutes

Ingredients:

- 279g potatoes, chopped, boiled & mashed
- 268g kale, chopped
- 1 garlic clove, minced
- 30ml milk
- Pepper
- Salt

Directions:

1. In a bowl, mix potatoes, kale, milk, garlic, pepper, and salt until well combined.
2. Insert a crisper plate in the Ninja Foodi air fryer baskets.
3. Make small balls from the potato mixture and place them both baskets.
4. Select zone 1 then select "air fry" mode and set the temperature to 390 degrees F for 15 minutes. Press "match" to match zone 2 settings to zone 1. Press "start/ stop" to begin. Turn halfway through.

Nutrition Info:

- (Per serving) Calories 90 | Fat 0.2g |Sodium 76mg | Carbs 19.4g | Fiber 2.8g | Sugar 1.2g | Protein 3.6g

Cauliflower Cheese Patties

Servings: 4 | Cooking Time: 10 Minutes

Ingredients:

- 2 eggs
- 200g cauliflower rice, microwave for 5 minutes
- 56g mozzarella cheese, shredded
- 22g parmesan cheese, grated
- 11g Mexican cheese, shredded
- ½ tsp onion powder
- 1 tsp dried basil
- 1 tsp garlic powder
- 33g breadcrumbs
- Pepper
- Salt

Directions:

1. Add cauliflower rice and remaining ingredients into the mixing bowl and mix until well combined.

2. Insert a crisper plate in the Ninja Foodi air fryer baskets.
3. Make patties from the cauliflower mixture and place them in both baskets.
4. Select zone 1, then select "air fry" mode and set the temperature to 390 degrees F for 10 minutes. Press "match" to match zone 2 settings to zone 1. Press "start/stop" to begin. Turn halfway through.

Nutrition Info:

• (Per serving) Calories 318 | Fat 18g |Sodium 951mg | Carbs 11.1g | Fiber 1.8g | Sugar 2.2g | Protein 25.6g

Avocado Fries With Sriracha Dip

Servings: 4 | Cooking Time: 6 Minutes

Ingredients:

- Avocado Fries
- 4 avocados, peeled and cut into sticks
- ¾ cup panko breadcrumbs
- ¼ cup flour
- 2 eggs, beaten
- ½ teaspoon garlic powder
- ½ teaspoon salt
- SRIRACHA-RANCH SAUCE
- ¼ cup ranch dressing
- 1 teaspoon sriracha sauce

Directions:

1. Mix flour with garlic powder and salt in a bowl.
2. Dredge the avocado sticks through the flour mixture.
3. Dip them in the eggs and coat them with breadcrumbs.
4. Place the coated fries in the air fryer baskets.
5. Return the air fryer basket 1 to Zone 1, and basket 2 to Zone 2 of the Ninja Foodi 2-Basket Air Fryer.
6. Choose the "Air Fry" mode for Zone 1 at 400 degrees F and 6 minutes of cooking time.
7. Select the "MATCH COOK" option to copy the settings for Zone 2.
8. Initiate cooking by pressing the START/PAUSE BUTTON.
9. Flip the fries once cooked halfway through.
10. Mix all the dipping sauce ingredients in a bowl.
11. Serve the fries with dipping sauce.

Nutrition Info:

• (Per serving) Calories 229 | Fat 1.9 |Sodium 567mg | Carbs 1.9g | Fiber 0.4g | Sugar 0.6g | Protein 11.8g

Potato Chips

Servings: 4 | Cooking Time: 16 Minutes

Ingredients:

- 2 large potatoes, peeled and sliced
- 1½ teaspoons salt
- 1½ teaspoons black pepper
- Oil for misting

Directions:

1. Soak potatoes in cold water for 30 minutes then drain.
2. Pat dry the potato slices and toss them with cracked pepper, salt and oil mist.
3. Spread the potatoes in the air fryer basket.
4. Return the air fryer basket 1 to Zone 1, and basket 2 to Zone 2 of the Ninja Foodi 2-Basket Air Fryer.
5. Choose the "Air Fry" mode for Zone 1 at 300 degrees F and 16 minutes of cooking time.
6. Select the "MATCH COOK" option to copy the settings for Zone 2.
7. Initiate cooking by pressing the START/PAUSE BUTTON.
8. Toss the fries once cooked halfway through.
9. Serve warm.

Nutrition Info:

• (Per serving) Calories 122 | Fat 1.8g |Sodium 794mg | Carbs 17g | Fiber 8.9g | Sugar 1.6g | Protein 14.9g

Tasty Sweet Potato Wedges

Servings: 4 | Cooking Time: 20 Minutes

Ingredients:

- 2 sweet potatoes, peel & cut into wedges
- 1 tbsp BBQ spice rub
- ½ tsp sweet paprika
- 1 tbsp olive oil
- Pepper
- Salt

Directions:

1. In a bowl, toss sweet potato wedges with sweet paprika, oil, BBQ spice rub, pepper, and salt.
2. Insert a crisper plate in the Ninja Foodi air fryer baskets.
3. Add sweet potato wedges in both baskets.
4. Select zone 1 then select "air fry" mode and set the temperature to 390 degrees F for 20 minutes. Press "match" to match zone 2 settings to zone 1. Press "start/stop" to begin. Turn halfway through.

Nutrition Info:

• (Per serving) Calories 87 | Fat 3.6g |Sodium 75mg | Carbs 13.2g | Fiber 2.1g | Sugar 2.8g | Protein 1.1g

Chicken Stuffed Mushrooms

Servings: 6 | Cooking Time: 15 Minutes.

Ingredients:

- 6 large fresh mushrooms, stems removed
- Stuffing:
- ½ cup chicken meat, cubed
- 1 (4 ounces) package cream cheese, softened
- ¼ lb. imitation crabmeat, flaked
- 1 cup butter
- 1 garlic clove, peeled and minced
- Black pepper and salt to taste
- Garlic powder to taste
- Crushed red pepper to taste

Directions:

1. Melt and heat butter in a skillet over medium heat.
2. Add chicken and sauté for 5 minutes.
3. Add in all the remaining ingredients for the stuffing.
4. Cook for 5 minutes, then turn off the heat.
5. Allow the mixture to cool. Stuff each mushroom with a tablespoon of this mixture.
6. Divide the stuffed mushrooms in the two crisper plates.
7. Return the crisper plate to the Ninja Foodi Dual Zone Air Fryer.
8. Choose the Air Fry mode for Zone 1 and set the temperature to 375 degrees F and the time to 15 minutes.
9. Select the "MATCH" button to copy the settings for Zone 2.
10. Initiate cooking by pressing the START/STOP button.
11. Serve warm.

Nutrition Info:

- (Per serving) Calories 180 | Fat 3.2g |Sodium 133mg | Carbs 32g | Fiber 1.1g | Sugar 1.8g | Protein 9g

Miso-glazed Shishito Peppers Charred Lemon Shishito Peppers

Servings:4 | Cooking Time: 10 Minutes

Ingredients:

- FOR THE MISO-GLAZED PEPPERS
- 2 tablespoons vegetable oil
- 2 tablespoons water
- 1 tablespoon white miso
- 1 teaspoon grated fresh ginger
- ½ pound shishito peppers
- FOR THE CHARRED LEMON PEPPERS
- ½ pound shishito peppers
- 1 lemon, cut into ⅛-inch-thick rounds
- 2 garlic cloves, minced
- 2 tablespoons vegetable oil
- ½ teaspoon kosher salt

Directions:

1. To prep the miso-glazed peppers: In a large bowl, mix the vegetable oil, water, miso, and ginger until well combined. Add the shishitos and toss to coat.
2. To prep the charred lemon peppers: In a large bowl, combine the shishitos, lemon slices, garlic, vegetable oil, and salt. Toss to coat.
3. To cook the peppers: Install a crisper plate in each of the two baskets. Place the miso-glazed peppers in the Zone 1 basket and insert the basket in the unit. Place the peppers with lemons in the Zone 2 basket and insert the basket in the unit.
4. Select Zone 1, select AIR FRY, set the temperature to 390°F, and set the time to 10 minutes. Select MATCH COOK to match Zone 2 settings to Zone 1.
5. Press START/PAUSE to begin cooking.
6. When both timers read 4 minutes, press START/PAUSE. Remove both baskets and shake well. Reinsert the baskets and press START/PAUSE to resume cooking.
7. When cooking is complete, serve immediately.

Nutrition Info:

- (Per serving) Calories: 165; Total fat: 14g; Saturated fat: 2g; Carbohydrates: 9g; Fiber: 2g; Protein: 2g; Sodium: 334mg

Crab Cake Poppers

Servings: 6 | Cooking Time: 10 Minutes

Ingredients:

- 1 egg, lightly beaten
- 453g lump crab meat, drained
- 1 tsp garlic, minced
- 1 tsp lemon juice
- 1 tsp old bay seasoning
- 30g almond flour
- 1 tsp Dijon mustard
- 28g mayonnaise
- Pepper
- Salt

Directions:

1. In a bowl, mix crab meat and remaining ingredients until well combined.
2. Make small balls from the crab meat mixture and place them on a plate.
3. Place the plate in the refrigerator for 50 minutes.
4. Insert a crisper plate in the Ninja Foodi air fryer baskets.
5. Place the prepared crab meatballs in both baskets.
6. Select zone 1 then select "air fry" mode and set the temperature to 360 degrees F for 10 minutes. Press "match" to match zone 2 settings to zone 1. Press "start/stop" to begin.

Nutrition Info:

• (Per serving) Calories 86 | Fat 8.5g |Sodium 615mg | Carbs 2.7g | Fiber 0.1g | Sugar 0.4g | Protein 12g

Mexican Jalapeno Poppers

Servings: 8 | Cooking Time: 5minutes

Ingredients:

- 5 jalapenos, cut in half & remove seeds
- ¼ tsp red pepper flakes, crushed
- 1 tsp onion powder
- 32g salsa
- 113g goat cheese
- 1 tsp garlic powder
- Pepper
- Salt

Directions:

1. In a small bowl, mix goat cheese, salsa, red pepper flakes, onion powder, garlic powder, pepper, and salt.
2. Stuff each jalapeno half with goat cheese mixture.
3. Insert a crisper plate in the Ninja Foodi air fryer baskets.
4. Place stuffed peppers in both baskets.
5. Select zone 1 then select "air fry" mode and set the temperature to 360 degrees F for 8 minutes—Press "match" to match zone 2 settings to zone 1. Press "start/stop" to begin.

Nutrition Info:

• (Per serving) Calories 112 | Fat 8.2g |Sodium 148mg | Carbs 2.6g | Fiber 0.6g | Sugar 1.5g | Protein 7.4g

Mac And Cheese Balls

Servings: 4 | Cooking Time: 20 Minutes

Ingredients:

- 1 cup panko breadcrumbs
- 4 cups prepared macaroni and cheese, refrigerated
- 3 tablespoons flour
- 1 teaspoon salt, divided
- 1 teaspoon ground black pepper, divided
- 1 teaspoon smoked paprika, divided
- ½ teaspoon garlic powder, divided
- 2 eggs
- 1 tablespoon milk
- ¼ cup ranch dressing, garlic aioli, or chipotle mayo, for dipping (optional)

Directions:

1. Preheat a conventional oven to 400 degrees F/ 200 degrees C.
2. Shake the breadcrumbs onto a baking sheet so that they're evenly distributed. Bake in the oven for 3 minutes, then shake and bake for an additional 1 to 2 minutes, or until toasted.
3. Form the chilled macaroni and cheese into golf ball-sized balls and set them aside.
4. Combine the flour, ½ teaspoon salt, ½ teaspoon black pepper, ½ teaspoon smoked paprika, and ¼ teaspoon garlic powder in a large mixing bowl.
5. In a small bowl, whisk together the eggs and milk.
6. Combine the breadcrumbs, remaining salt, pepper, paprika, and garlic powder in a mixing bowl.
7. To coat the macaroni and cheese balls, roll them in the flour mixture, then the egg mixture, and then the breadcrumb mixture.
8. Place a crisper plate in each drawer. Put the cheese balls in a single layer in each drawer. Insert the drawers into the unit.
9. Select zone 1, then AIR FRY, then set the temperature to 360 degrees F/ 180 degrees C with an 8-minute timer. To match zone 2 settings to zone 1, choose MATCH. To begin, select START/STOP.
10. Serve and enjoy!

Nutrition Info:

• (Per serving) Calories 489 | Fat 15.9g | Sodium 1402mg | Carbs 69.7g | Fiber 2.5g | Sugar 4g | Protein 16.9g

Crispy Popcorn Shrimp

Servings: 4 | Cooking Time: 6 Minutes

Ingredients:

- 170g shrimp, peeled and diced
- ½ cup breadcrumbs
- Salt and black pepper to taste
- 2 eggs, beaten

Directions:

1. Mix breadcrumbs with black pepper and salt in a bowl.
2. Dip the shrimp pieces in the eggs and coat each with breadcrumbs.
3. Divide the shrimp popcorn into the 2 Air Fryer baskets.
4. Return the air fryer basket 1 to Zone 1, and basket 2 to Zone 2 of the Ninja Foodi 2-Basket Air Fryer.
5. Choose the "Air Fry" mode for Zone 1 at 400 degrees F and 6 minutes of cooking time.
6. Select the "MATCH COOK" option to copy the settings for Zone 2.
7. Initiate cooking by pressing the START/PAUSE BUTTON.
8. Serve warm.

Nutrition Info:

• (Per serving) Calories 180 | Fat 3.2g |Sodium 133mg | Carbs 32g | Fiber 1.1g | Sugar 1.8g | Protein 9g

Cheddar Quiche

Servings:2 | Cooking Time:12

Ingredients:

- 4 eggs, organic
- 1-1/4 cup heavy cream
- Salt, pinch
- ½ cup broccoli florets
- ½ cup cheddar cheese, shredded and for sprinkling

Directions:

1. Take a Pyrex pitcher and crack two eggs in it.
2. And fill it with heavy cream, about half the way up.
3. Add in the salt and then add in the broccoli and pour this into two quiche dishes, and top it with shredded cheddar cheese.
4. Now divide it between both zones of baskets.
5. For zone 1, set the time to 10-12 minutes at 325 degrees F.
6. Select the MATCH button for the zone 2 basket.
7. Once done, serve hot.

Nutrition Info:

- (Per serving) Calories 454| Fat40g | Sodium 406mg | Carbs 4.2g | Fiber 0.6g| Sugar1.3 g | Protein 20g

Garlic Bread

Servings: 4 | Cooking Time: 10 Minutes

Ingredients:

- ½ loaf of bread
- 3 tablespoons butter, softened
- 3 garlic cloves, minced
- ½ teaspoon Italian seasoning
- Small pinch of red pepper flakes
- Optional
- ¼ cup shredded mozzarella cheese
- Freshly grated parmesan cheese
- Chopped fresh parsley for serving/topping

Directions:

1. Slice the bread in half horizontally or as appropriate to fit inside the air fryer.
2. Combine the softened butter, garlic, Italian seasoning, and red pepper flakes in a mixing bowl.
3. Brush the garlic butter mixture evenly over the bread.
4. Place a crisper plate in each drawer. Place the bread pieces into each drawer. Insert the drawers into the unit.
5. Select zone 1, then AIR FRY, then set the temperature to 360 degrees F/ 180 degrees C with a 6-minute timer. To match zone 2 settings to zone 1, choose MATCH. To begin, select START/STOP.
6. Remove the garlic bread from your air fryer, slice, and serve!

Nutrition Info:

- (Per serving) Calories 150 | Fat 8.2g | Sodium 208mg | Carbs 14.3g | Fiber 2.3g | Sugar 1.2g | Protein 4.9g

Tofu Veggie Meatballs

Servings: 4 | Cooking Time: 10minutes

Ingredients:

- 122g firm tofu, drained
- 50g breadcrumbs
- 37g bamboo shoots, thinly sliced
- 22g carrots, shredded & steamed
- 1 tsp garlic powder
- 1 ½ tbsp soy sauce
- 2 tbsp cornstarch
- 3 dried shitake mushrooms, soaked & chopped
- Pepper
- Salt

Directions:

1. Add tofu and remaining ingredients into the food processor and process until well combined.
2. Insert a crisper plate in the Ninja Foodi air fryer baskets.
3. Make small balls from the tofu mixture and place them in both baskets.
4. Select zone 1, then select "air fry" mode and set the temperature to 380 degrees F for 10 minutes. Press "match" to match zone 2 settings to zone 1. Press "start/stop" to begin. Turn halfway through.

Nutrition Info:

- (Per serving) Calories 125 | Fat 1.8g |Sodium 614mg | Carbs 23.4g | Fiber 2.5g | Sugar 3.8g | Protein 5.3g

Beef Jerky Pineapple Jerky

Servings:8 | Cooking Time: 6 To 12 Hours

Ingredients:

- FOR THE BEEF JERKY
- ½ cup reduced-sodium soy sauce
- ¼ cup pineapple juice
- 1 tablespoon dark brown sugar
- 1 tablespoon Worcestershire sauce
- ½ teaspoon smoked paprika
- ¼ teaspoon freshly ground black pepper
- ¼ teaspoon red pepper flakes
- 1 pound beef bottom round, trimmed of excess fat, cut into ¼-inch-thick slices
- FOR THE PINEAPPLE JERKY
- 1 pound pineapple, cut into ⅛-inch-thick rounds, pat dry
- 1 teaspoon chili powder (optional)

Directions:

1. To prep the beef jerky: In a large zip-top bag, combine the soy sauce, pineapple juice, brown sugar, Worcestershire sauce, smoked paprika, black pepper, and red pepper flakes.
2. Add the beef slices, seal the bag, and toss to coat the

meat in the marinade. Refrigerate overnight or for at least 8 hours.
3. Remove the beef slices and discard the marinade. Using a paper towel, pat the slices dry to remove excess marinade.
4. To prep the pineapple jerky: Sprinkle the pineapple with chili powder (if using).
5. To dehydrate the jerky: Arrange half of the beef slices in a single layer in the Zone 1 basket, making sure they do not overlap. Place a crisper plate on top of the beef slices and arrange the remaining slices in a single layer on top of the crisper plate. Insert the basket in the unit.
6. Repeat this process with the pineapple in the Zone 2 basket and insert the basket in the unit.
7. Select Zone 1, select DEHYDRATE, set the temperature to 150°F, and set the time to 8 hours.
8. Select Zone 2, select DEHYDRATE, set the temperature to 135°F, and set the time to 12 hours.
9. Press START/PAUSE to begin cooking.
10. When the Zone 1 timer reads 2 hours, press START/PAUSE. Remove the basket and check the beef jerky for doneness. If necessary, reinsert the basket and press START/PAUSE to resume cooking.

Nutrition Info:

• (Per serving) Calories: 171; Total fat: 6.5g; Saturated fat: 2g; Carbohydrates: 2g; Fiber: 0g; Protein: 25g; Sodium: 369mg

Chicken Tenders

Servings:3 | Cooking Time:12

Ingredients:

- 1 pound of chicken tender
- Salt and black pepper, to taste
- 1 cup Panko bread crumbs
- 2 cups Italian bread crumbs
- 1 cup parmesan cheese
- 2 eggs
- Oil spray, for greasing

Directions:

1. Sprinkle the tenders with salt and black pepper.
2. In a medium bowl mix Panko bread crumbs with Italian breadcrumbs.
3. Add salt, pepper, and parmesan cheese.
4. Crack two eggs in a bowl.
5. First, put the chicken tender in eggs.
6. Now dredge the tender in a bowl and coat the tender well with crumbs.
7. Line both of the baskets of the air fryer with parchment paper.
8. At the end spray the tenders with oil spray.
9. Divided the tenders between the baskets of Ninja Foodie 2-Basket Air Fryer.
10. Set zone 1 basket to AIR FRY mode at 350 degrees F for 12 minutes.
11. Select the MATCH button for the zone 2 basket.
12. Once it's done, serve.

Nutrition Info:

• (Per serving) Calories558 | Fat23.8g | Sodium872 mg | Carbs 20.9g | Fiber1.7 g| Sugar2.2 g | Protein 63.5g

Stuffed Bell Peppers

Servings:3 | Cooking Time:16

Ingredients:

- 6 large bell peppers
- 1-1/2 cup cooked rice
- 2 cups cheddar cheese

Directions:

1. Cut the bell peppers in half lengthwise and remove all the seeds.
2. Fill the cavity of each bell pepper with cooked rice.
3. Divide the bell peppers amongst the two zones of the air fryer basket.
4. Set the time for zone 1 for 200 degrees for 10 minutes.
5. Select MATCH button of zone 2 basket.
6. Afterward, take out the baskets and sprinkle cheese on top.
7. Set the time for zone 1 for 200 degrees for 6 minutes.
8. Select MATCH button of zone 2 basket.
9. Once it's done, serve.

Nutrition Info:

• (Per serving) Calories 605| Fat 26g | Sodium477 mg | Carbs68.3 g | Fiber4 g| Sugar 12.5g | Protein25.6 g

Grill Cheese Sandwich

Servings:2 | Cooking Time:10

Ingredients:

- 4 slices of white bread slices
- 2 tablespoons of butter, melted
- 2 slices of sharp cheddar
- 2 slices of Swiss cheese
- 2 slices of mozzarella cheese

Directions:

1. Brush melted butter on one side of all the bread slices and then top the 2 bread slices with slices of cheddar, Swiss, and mozzarella, one slice per bread.
2. Top it with the other slice to make a sandwich.
3. Divide it between two baskets of the air fryer.
4. Turn on AIR FRY mode for zone 1 basket at 350 degrees F for 10 minutes.
5. Use the MATCH button for the second zone.
6. Once done, serve.

Nutrition Info:

• (Per serving) Calories 577 | Fat38g | Sodium 1466mg | Carbs 30.5g | Fiber 1.1g| Sugar 6.5g | Protein 27.6g

Breakfast Recipes

Strawberry Baked Oats Chocolate Peanut Butter Baked Oats

Servings:12 | Cooking Time: 15 Minutes

Ingredients:

- FOR THE STRAWBERRY OATS
- 1 cup whole milk
- 1 cup heavy (whipping) cream
- ½ cup maple syrup
- 2 teaspoons vanilla extract
- 2 large eggs
- 2 cups old-fashioned oats
- 2 teaspoons baking powder
- ½ teaspoon ground cinnamon
- ¼ teaspoon kosher salt
- 1½ cups diced strawberries
- FOR THE CHOCOLATE PEANUT BUTTER OATS
- 2 very ripe bananas
- ½ cup maple syrup
- ¼ cup unsweetened cocoa powder
- 2 teaspoons vanilla extract
- 2 teaspoons baking powder
- 2 large eggs
- ½ teaspoon kosher salt
- 2 cups old-fashioned oats
- 2 tablespoons peanut butter

Directions:

1. To prep the strawberry oats: In a large bowl, combine the milk, cream, maple syrup, vanilla, and eggs. Stir in the oats, baking powder, cinnamon, and salt until fully combined. Fold in the strawberries.
2. To prep the chocolate peanut butter oats: In a large bowl, mash the banana with a fork. Stir in the maple syrup, cocoa powder, vanilla, baking powder, and salt until smooth. Beat in the eggs. Stir in the oats until everything is combined.
3. To bake the oats: Place the strawberry oatmeal in the Zone 1 basket and insert the basket in the unit. Place the chocolate peanut butter oatmeal in the Zone 2 basket. Add ½ teaspoon dollops of peanut butter on top and insert the basket in the unit.
4. Select Zone 1, select BAKE, set the temperature to 320°F, and set the time to 15 minutes. Select MATCH COOK to match Zone 2 settings to Zone 1.
5. Press START/PAUSE to begin cooking.
6. When cooking is complete, serve each oatmeal in a shallow bowl.

Nutrition Info:

- (Per serving) Calories: 367; Total fat: 19g; Saturated fat: 11g; Carbohydrates: 42g; Fiber: 3.5g; Protein: 8g; Sodium: 102mg

Brussels Sprouts Potato Hash

Servings: 4 | Cooking Time: 10 Minutes

Ingredients:

- 455g Brussels sprouts
- 1 small to medium red onion
- 227g baby red potatoes
- 2 tablespoons avocado oil
- ½ teaspoon salt
- ½ teaspoon black pepper

Directions:

1. Peel and boil potatoes in salted water for 15 minutes until soft.
2. Drain and allow them to cool down then dice.
3. Shred Brussels sprouts and toss them with potatoes and the rest of the ingredients.
4. Divide this veggies hash mixture in both of the air fryer baskets.
5. Return the air fryer basket 1 to Zone 1, and basket 2 to Zone 2 of the Ninja Foodi 2-Basket Air Fryer.
6. Choose the "Air Fry" mode for Zone 1 with 375 degrees F temperature and 10 minutes of cooking time.
7. Select the "MATCH COOK" option to copy the settings for Zone 2.
8. Initiate cooking by pressing the START/PAUSE BUTTON.
9. Shake the veggies once cooked halfway through.
10. Serve warm.

Nutrition Info:

- (Per serving) Calories 305 | Fat 25g |Sodium 532mg | Carbs 2.3g | Fiber 0.4g | Sugar 2g | Protein 18.3g

Breakfast Sausage Omelet

Servings:2 | Cooking Time:8

Ingredients:

- ¼ pound breakfast sausage, cooked and crumbled
- 4 eggs, beaten
- ½ cup pepper Jack cheese blend
- 2 tablespoons green bell pepper, sliced
- 1 green onion, chopped
- 1 pinch cayenne pepper
- Cooking spray

Directions:

1. Take a bowl and whisk eggs in it along with crumbled sausage, pepper Jack cheese, green onions, red bell pepper, and cayenne pepper.
2. Mix it all well.
3. Take two cake pans that fit inside the air fryer and grease it with oil spray.
4. Divide the omelet mixture between cake pans.
5. Put the cake pans inside both of the Ninja Foodie 2-Basket Air Fryer baskets.
6. Turn on the BAKE function of the zone 1 basket and let it cook for 15-20 minutes at 310 degrees F.
7. Select MATCH button for zone 2 basket.
8. Once the cooking cycle completes, take out, and serve hot, as a delicious breakfast.

Nutrition Info:

- (Per serving) Calories 691| Fat52.4g | Sodium1122 mg | Carbs 13.3g | Fiber 1.8g| Sugar 7g | Protein 42g

Bacon And Egg Omelet

Servings:2 | Cooking Time:10

Ingredients:

- 2 eggs, whisked
- ½ teaspoon of chopped tomatoes
- Sea Salt and black pepper, to taste
- 2 teaspoons of almond milk
- 1 teaspoon of cilantro, chopped
- 1 small green chili, chopped
- 4 slices of bacon

Directions:

1. Take a bowl and whisk eggs in it.
2. Then add green chili salt, black pepper, cilantro, almond milk, and chopped tomatoes.
3. Oil greases the ramekins.
4. Pour this into ramekins.
5. Put the bacon in the zone 1 basket and ramekins in zone 2 basket of the Ninja Foodie 2-Basket Air Fryer.
6. Now for zone 1, set it to AIR FRY mode at 400 degrees F for 10 minutes
7. And for zone 2, set it 350 degrees for 10 minutes in AIR FRY mode.
8. Press the Smart finish button and press start, it will finish both at the same time.
9. Once done, serve and enjoy.

Nutrition Info:

- (Per serving) Calories 285| Fat 21.5g| Sodium1000 mg | Carbs 2.2g | Fiber 0.1g| Sugar1 g | Protein 19.7g

Breakfast Cheese Sandwich

Servings: 2 | Cooking Time: 8 Minutes

Ingredients:

- 4 bread slices
- 2 provolone cheese slice
- ¼ tsp dried basil
- 2 tbsp mayonnaise
- 2 Monterey jack cheese slice
- 2 cheddar cheese slice
- ¼ tsp dried oregano

Directions:

1. In a small bowl, mix mayonnaise, basil, and oregano.
2. Spread mayonnaise on one side of the two bread slices.
3. Top two bread slices with cheddar cheese, provolone cheese, Monterey jack cheese slice, and cover with remaining bread slices.
4. Insert a crisper plate in the Ninja Foodi air fryer baskets.
5. Place sandwiches in both baskets.
6. Select zone 1, then select "air fry" mode and set the temperature to 390 degrees F for 8 minutes. Press "match" to match zone 2 settings to zone 1. Press "start/stop" to begin. Turn halfway through.

Nutrition Info:

- (Per serving) Calories 421 | Fat 30.7g |Sodium 796mg | Carbs 13.9g | Fiber 0.5g | Sugar 2.2g | Protein 22.5g

Blueberry Coffee Cake And Maple Sausage Patties

Servings:6 | Cooking Time: 25 Minutes

Ingredients:

- FOR THE COFFEE CAKE
- 6 tablespoons unsalted butter, at room temperature, divided
- ⅓ cup granulated sugar
- 1 large egg
- 1 teaspoon vanilla extract
- ¼ cup whole milk
- 1½ cups all-purpose flour, divided
- 1 teaspoon baking powder
- ¼ teaspoon salt
- 1 cup blueberries
- ¼ cup packed light brown sugar
- ½ teaspoon ground cinnamon
- FOR THE SAUSAGE PATTIES
- ½ pound ground pork
- 2 tablespoons maple syrup
- ½ teaspoon dried sage
- ½ teaspoon dried thyme
- 1½ teaspoons kosher salt
- ½ teaspoon crushed fennel seeds
- ½ teaspoon red pepper flakes (optional)
- ¼ teaspoon freshly ground black pepper

Directions:

1. To prep the coffee cake: In a large bowl, cream together 4 tablespoons of butter with the granulated sugar. Beat in the egg, vanilla, and milk.
2. Stir in 1 cup of flour, along with the baking soda and salt, to form a thick batter. Fold in the blueberries.
3. In a second bowl, mix the remaining 2 tablespoons of butter, remaining ½ cup of flour, the brown sugar, and cinnamon to form a dry crumbly mixture.
4. To prep the sausage patties: In a large bowl, mix the pork, maple syrup, sage, thyme, salt, fennel seeds, red pepper flakes (if using), and black pepper until just combined.
5. Divide the mixture into 6 equal patties about ½ inch thick.
6. To cook the coffee cake and sausage patties: Spread the cake batter into the Zone 1 basket, top with the crumble mixture, and insert the basket in the unit. Install a crisper plate in the Zone 2 basket, add the sausage patties in a single layer, and insert the basket in the unit.
7. Select Zone 1, select BAKE, set the temperature to 350°F, and set the time to 25 minutes.
8. Select Zone 2, select AIR FRY, set the temperature to 375°F, and set the time to 12 minutes. Select SMART FINISH.
9. Press START/PAUSE to begin cooking.
10. When the Zone 2 timer reads 6 minutes, press START/PAUSE. Remove the basket and use silicone-tipped tongs to flip the sausage patties. Reinsert the basket and press START/PAUSE to resume cooking.
11. When cooking is complete, let the coffee cake cool for at least 5 minutes, then cut into 6 slices. Serve warm or at room temperature with the sausage patties.

Nutrition Info:

- (Per serving) Calories: 395; Total fat: 15g; Saturated fat: 8g; Carbohydrates: 53g; Fiber: 1.5g; Protein: 14g; Sodium: 187mg

Morning Egg Rolls

Servings: 6 | Cooking Time: 13 Minutes.

Ingredients:

- 2 eggs
- 2 tablespoons milk
- Salt, to taste
- Black pepper, to taste
- ½ cup shredded cheddar cheese
- 2 sausage patties
- 6 egg roll wrappers
- 1 tablespoon olive oil
- 1 cup water

Directions:

1. Grease a small skillet with some olive oil and place it over medium heat.
2. Add sausage patties and cook them until brown.
3. Chop the cooked patties into small pieces. Beat eggs with salt, black pepper, and milk in a mixing bowl.
4. Grease the same skillet with 1 teaspoon of olive oil and pour the egg mixture into it.
5. Stir cook to make scrambled eggs.
6. Add sausage, mix well and remove the skillet from the heat.
7. Spread an egg roll wrapper on the working surface in a diamond shape position.
8. Add a tablespoon of cheese at the bottom third of the roll wrapper.
9. Top the cheese with egg mixture and wet the edges of the wrapper with water.
10. Fold the two corners of the wrapper and roll it, then seal the edges.
11. Repeat the same steps and divide the rolls in the two crisper plates.
12. Return the crisper plates to the Ninja Foodi Dual Zone Air Fryer.
13. Choose the Air Fry mode for Zone 1 and set the temperature to 375 degrees F and the time to 13 minutes.
14. Select the "MATCH" button to copy the settings for Zone 2.

15. Initiate cooking by pressing the START/STOP button.
16. Flip the rolls after 8 minutes and continue cooking for another 5 minutes.
17. Serve warm and fresh.

Nutrition Info:

• (Per serving) Calories 282 | Fat 15g |Sodium 526mg | Carbs 20g | Fiber 0.6g | Sugar 3.3g | Protein 16g

Sweet Potato Sausage Hash

Servings: 4 | Cooking Time: 20 Minutes

Ingredients:

• 1½ pounds sweet potato, peeled and diced into ½-inch pieces
• 1 tablespoon minced garlic
• 1 teaspoon kosher salt plus more, as desired
• Ground black pepper, as desired
• 2 tablespoons canola oil
• 1 tablespoon dried sage
• 1-pound uncooked mild ground breakfast sausage
• ½ large onion, peeled and diced
• ½ teaspoon ground cinnamon
• 1 teaspoon chili powder
• 4 large eggs, poached or fried (optional)

Directions:

1. Toss the sweet potatoes with the garlic, salt, pepper, and canola oil in a mixing bowl.
2. Install the crisper plate in the zone 1 drawer, fill it with the sweet potato mixture, and insert the drawer in the unit.
3. Place the ground sausage in the zone 2 drawer (without the crisper plate) and place it in the unit.
4. Select zone 1, then AIR FRY, and set the temperature to 400 degrees F/ 200 degrees C with a 30-minute timer.
5. Select zone 2, then ROAST, then set the temperature to 400 degrees F/ 200 degrees C with a 20-minute timer. SYNC is the option to choose. To begin cooking, press the START/STOP button.
6. When the zone 1 and zone 2 times have reached 10 minutes, press START/STOP and remove the drawers from the unit. Shake each for 10 seconds.
7. Half of the sage should be added to the zone 1 drawer.
8. Add the onion to the zone 2 drawer and mix to incorporate. To continue cooking, press START/STOP and reinsert the drawers.
9. Remove both drawers from the unit once the cooking is finished and add the potatoes to the sausage mixture. Mix in the cinnamon, sage, chili powder, and salt until thoroughly combined.
10. When the hash is done, stir it and serve it right away with a poached or fried egg on top, if desired.

Nutrition Info:

• (Per serving) Calories 491 | Fat 19.5g | Sodium 736mg | Carbs 51g | Fiber 8g | Sugar 2g | Protein 26.3

Egg And Avocado In The Ninja Foodi

Servings:2 | Cooking Time:12

Ingredients:

• 2 Avocados, pitted and cut in half
• Garlic salt, to taste
• Cooking for greasing
• 4 eggs
• ¼ teaspoon of Paprika powder, for sprinkling
• 1/3 cup parmesan cheese, crumbled
• 6 bacon strips, raw

Directions:

1. First cut the avocado in half and pit it.
2. Now scoop out the flesh from the avocado and keep intact some of it
3. Crack one egg in each hole of avocado and sprinkle paprika and garlic salt
4. Top it with cheese at the end.
5. Now put it into tin foils and then put it in the air fryer zone basket 1
6. Put bacon strips in zone 2 basket.
7. Now for zone 1, set it to AIR FRY mode at 350 degrees F for 10 minutes
8. And for zone 2, set it 400 degrees for 12 minutes AIR FRY mode.
9. Press the Smart finish button and press start, it will finish both at the same time.
10. Once done, serve and enjoy.

Nutrition Info:

• (Per serving) Calories609 | Fat53.2g | Sodium 335mg | Carbs 18.1g | Fiber13.5g | Sugar 1.7g | Protein 21.3g

Cornbread

Servings: 6 | Cooking Time: 15 Minutes

Ingredients:

• 1 cup cornmeal
• 1 cup all-purpose flour
• 1 tablespoon sugar
• 2 teaspoons baking powder
• ½ teaspoon baking soda
• ½ teaspoon salt
• 1 stick butter melted
• 1½ cups buttermilk
• 2 eggs
• 113g diced chiles

Directions:

1. Mix cornmeal with flour, sugar, baking powder, baking soda, salt, butter, milk, eggs and chiles in a bowl until smooth.

2. Spread this mixture in two greased 4-inch baking pans.
3. Place one pan in each air fryer basket.
4. Return the air fryer basket 1 to Zone 1, and basket 2 to Zone 2 of the Ninja Foodi 2-Basket Air Fryer.
5. Choose the "Air Fry" mode for Zone 1 at 330 degrees F and 15 minutes of cooking time.
6. Select the "MATCH COOK" option to copy the settings for Zone 2.
7. Initiate cooking by pressing the START/PAUSE BUTTON.
8. Slice and serve.

Nutrition Info:

• (Per serving) Calories 199 | Fat 11.1g |Sodium 297mg | Carbs 14.9g | Fiber 1g | Sugar 2.5g | Protein 9.9g

Pumpkin French Toast Casserole With Sweet And Spicy Twisted Bacon

Servings:4 | Cooking Time: 35 Minutes

Ingredients:

- FOR THE FRENCH TOAST CASSEROLE
- 3 large eggs
- 1 cup unsweetened almond milk
- 1 cup canned unsweetened pumpkin puree
- 2 teaspoons pumpkin pie spice
- ¼ cup packed light brown sugar
- 1 teaspoon vanilla extract
- 6 cups French bread cubes
- 1 teaspoon vegetable oil
- ¼ cup maple syrup
- FOR THE BACON
- 2 tablespoons light brown sugar
- ⅛ teaspoon cayenne pepper
- 8 slices bacon

Directions:

1. To prep the French toast casserole: In a shallow bowl, whisk together the eggs, almond milk, pumpkin puree, pumpkin pie spice, brown sugar, and vanilla.
2. Add the bread cubes to the egg mixture, making sure the bread is fully coated in the custard. Let sit for at least 10 minutes to allow the bread to soak up the custard.
3. To prep the bacon: In a small bowl, combine the brown sugar and cayenne.
4. Arrange the bacon on a cutting board in a single layer. Evenly sprinkle the strips with the brown sugar mixture. Fold the bacon strip in half lengthwise. Hold one end of the bacon steady and twist the other end so the bacon resembles a straw.
5. To cook the casserole and bacon: Brush the Zone 1 basket with the oil. Pour the French toast casserole into the Zone 1 basket, drizzle with maple syrup, and insert the basket in the unit. Install a crisper plate in the Zone 2 basket, add the bacon twists in a single layer, and insert the basket in the unit. For the best fit, arrange the bacon twists across the unit, front to back.
6. Select Zone 1, select BAKE, set the temperature to 330°F, and set the time to 35 minutes.
7. Select Zone 2, select AIR FRY, set the temperature to 400°F, and set the time to 12 minutes. Select SMART FINISH.
8. Press START/PAUSE to begin cooking.
9. When cooking is complete, transfer the bacon to a plate lined with paper towels. Let cool for 2 to 3 minutes before serving with the French toast casserole.

Nutrition Info:

• (Per serving) Calories: 601; Total fat: 28g; Saturated fat: 9g; Carbohydrates: 67g; Fiber: 2.5g; Protein: 17g; Sodium: 814mg

Egg White Muffins

Servings: 8 | Cooking Time: 10 Minutes

Ingredients:

- 4 slices center-cut bacon, cut into strips
- 4 ounces baby bella mushrooms, roughly chopped
- 2 ounces sun-dried tomatoes
- 2 tablespoon sliced black olives
- 2 tablespoons grated or shredded parmesan
- 2 tablespoons shredded mozzarella
- ¼ teaspoon black pepper
- ¾ cup liquid egg whites
- 2 tablespoons liquid egg whites

Directions:

1. Heat a saucepan with a little oil, add the bacon and mushrooms and cook until fully cooked and crispy, about 6–8 minutes.
2. While the bacon and mushrooms cook, mix the ¾ cup liquid egg whites, sun-dried tomato, olives, parmesan, mozzarella, and black pepper together in a large bowl.
3. Add the cooked bacon and mushrooms to the tomato and olive mixture, stirring everything together.
4. Spoon the mixture into muffin molds, followed by 2 tablespoons of egg whites over the top.
5. Place half the muffins mold in zone 1 and half in zone 2, then insert the drawers into the unit.
6. Select zone 1, select AIR FRY, set temperature to 390 degrees F/ 200 degrees C, and set time to 22 minutes.
7. Select MATCH to match zone 2 settings to zone 1. Press the START/STOP button to begin cooking.
8. When cooking is complete, remove the molds and enjoy!

Nutrition Info:

• (Per serving) Calories 104 | Fat 5.6g | Sodium 269mg | Carbs 3.5g | Fiber 0.8g | Sugar 0.3g | Protein 10.3g

Lemon-cream Cheese Danishes Cherry Danishes

Servings:4 | Cooking Time: 15 Minutes

Ingredients:

- FOR THE CREAM CHEESE DANISHES
- 1 ounce (2 tablespoons) cream cheese, at room temperature
- 1 teaspoon granulated sugar
- ¼ teaspoon freshly squeezed lemon juice
- ⅛ teaspoon vanilla extract
- ½ sheet frozen puff pastry, thawed
- 2 tablespoons lemon curd
- 1 large egg yolk
- 1 tablespoon water
- FOR THE CHERRY DANISHES
- ½ sheet frozen puff pastry, thawed
- 2 tablespoons cherry preserves
- 1 teaspoon coarse sanding sugar

Directions:

1. To prep the cream cheese Danishes: In a small bowl, mix the cream cheese, granulated sugar, lemon juice, and vanilla.
2. Cut the puff pastry sheet into 2 squares. Cut a ½-inch-wide strip from each side of the pastry. Brush the edges of the pastry square with water, then layer the strips along the edges, pressing gently to adhere and form a border around the outside of the pastry.
3. Divide the cream cheese mixture between the two pastries, then top each with 1 tablespoon of lemon curd.
4. In a second small bowl, whisk together the egg yolk and water (this will be used for the cherry Danishes, too). Brush the exposed edges of the pastry with half the egg wash.
5. To prep the cherry Danishes: Cut the puff pastry sheet into 2 squares. Cut a ½-inch-wide strip from each side of the pastry. Brush the edges of the pastry square with water, then layer the strips along the edges, pressing gently to adhere and form a border around the outside of the pastry.
6. Spoon 1 tablespoon of cherry preserves into the center of each pastry.
7. Brush the exposed edges of the pastry with the remaining egg wash, then sprinkle with the sanding sugar.
8. To cook both Danishes: Install a crisper plate in each of the two baskets. Place the cream cheese Danishes in the Zone 1 basket and insert the basket in the unit. Place the cherry Danishes in the Zone 2 basket and insert the basket in the unit.
9. Select Zone 1, select AIR FRY, set the temperature to 330°F, and set the time to 15 minutes. Select MATCH COOK to match Zone 2 settings to Zone 1.
10. Press START/PAUSE to begin cooking.
11. When cooking is complete, transfer the Danishes to a wire rack to cool. Serve warm.

Nutrition Info:

- (Per serving) Calories: 415; Total fat: 24g; Saturated fat: 12g; Carbohydrates: 51g; Fiber: 1.5g; Protein: 7g; Sodium: 274mg

Breakfast Bacon

Servings: 4 | Cooking Time: 14 Minutes.

Ingredients:

- ½ lb. bacon slices

Directions:

1. Spread half of the bacon slices in each of the crisper plate evenly in a single layer.
2. Return the crisper plate to the Ninja Foodi Dual Zone Air Fryer.
3. Choose the Air Fry mode for Zone 1 and set the temperature to 390 degrees F and the time to 14 minutes.
4. Select the "MATCH" button to copy the settings for Zone 2.
5. Initiate cooking by pressing the START/STOP button.
6. Flip the crispy bacon once cooked halfway through, then resume cooking.
7. Serve.

Nutrition Info:

- (Per serving) Calories 273 | Fat 22g |Sodium 517mg | Carbs 3.3g | Fiber 0.2g | Sugar 1.4g | Protein 16.1g

Easy Pancake Doughnuts

Servings: 8 | Cooking Time: 9 Minutes

Ingredients:

- 2 eggs
- 50g sugar
- 125ml vegetable oil
- 240g pancake mix
- 1 ½ tbsp cinnamon

Directions:

1. In a bowl, mix pancake mix, eggs, cinnamon, sugar, and oil until well combined.
2. Pour the doughnut mixture into the silicone doughnut moulds.
3. Insert a crisper plate in Ninja Foodi air fryer baskets.
4. Place doughnut moulds in both baskets.
5. Select zone 1 then select "air fry" mode and set the temperature to 355 degrees F for 9 minutes. Press "match" to match zone 2 settings to zone 1. Press "start/stop" to begin.

Nutrition Info:

- (Per serving) Calories 163 | Fat 14.7g |Sodium 16mg | Carbs 7.4g | Fiber 0.7g | Sugar 6.4g | Protein 1.4g

Egg With Baby Spinach

Servings:4 | Cooking Time:12

Ingredients:

- Nonstick spray, for greasing ramekins
- 2 tablespoons olive oil
- 6 ounces baby spinach
- 2 garlic cloves, minced
- 1/3 teaspoon kosher salt
- 6-8 large eggs
- ½ cup half and half
- Salt and black pepper, to taste
- 8 Sourdough bread slices, toasted

Directions:

1. Grease 4 ramekins with oil spray and set aside for further use.
2. Take a skillet and heat oil in it.
3. Then cook spinach for 2 minutes and add garlic and salt black pepper.
4. Let it simmer for2more minutes.
5. Once the spinach is wilted, transfer it to a plate.
6. Whisk an egg into a small bowl.
7. Add in the spinach.
8. Whisk it well and then pour half and half.
9. Divide this mixture between 4 ramekins and remember not to overfill it to the top, leave a little space on top.
10. Put the ramekins in zone 1 and zone 2 baskets of the Ninja Foodie 2-Basket Air Fryer.
11. Press start and set zone 1 to AIR fry it at 350 degrees F for 8-12 minutes.
12. Press the MATCH button for zone 2.
13. Once it's cooked and eggs are done, serve with sourdough bread slices.

Nutrition Info:

- (Per serving) Calories 404| Fat 19.6g| Sodium 761mg | Carbs 40.1g | Fiber 2.5g| Sugar 2.5g | Protein 19.2g

Yellow Potatoes With Eggs

Servings:2 | Cooking Time:35

Ingredients:

- 1 pound of Dutch yellow potatoes, quartered
- 1 red bell pepper, chopped
- Salt and black pepper, to taste
- 1 green bell pepper, chopped
- 2 teaspoons of olive oil
- 2 teaspoons of garlic powder
- 1 teaspoon of onion powder
- 1 egg
- ¼ teaspoon of butter

Directions:

1. Toss together diced potatoes, green pepper, red pepper, salt, black pepper, and olive oil along with garlic powder and onion powder.
2. Put in the zone 1 basket of the air fryer.
3. Take ramekin and grease it with oil spray.
4. Whisk egg in a bowl and add salt and pepper along with ½ teaspoon of butter.
5. Pour egg into a ramekin and place it in a zone 2 basket.
6. Now start cooking and set a timer for zone 1 basket to 30-35 minutes at 400 degrees at AIR FRY mode.
7. Now for zone 2, set it on AIR FRY mode at 350 degrees F for 8-10 minutes.
8. Press the Smart finish button and press start, it will finish both at the same time.
9. Once done, serve and enjoy.

Nutrition Info:

- (Per serving) Calories252 | Fat7.5g | Sodium 37mg | Carbs 40g | Fiber3.9g | Sugar 7g | Protein 6.7g

Healthy Oatmeal Muffins

Servings: 6 | Cooking Time: 17 Minutes

Ingredients:

- 1 egg
- ¼ tsp ground ginger
- 1 tsp ground cinnamon
- ½ tsp baking soda
- ½ tsp baking powder
- 55g brown sugar
- ½ tsp vanilla
- 2 tbsp butter, melted
- 125g applesauce
- 61ml milk
- 68gm whole wheat flour
- 100gm quick oats
- Pinch of salt

Directions:

1. In a mixing bowl, mix together all dry the ingredients.
2. In a separate bowl, add the remaining ingredients and mix well.
3. Add the dry ingredients mixture into the wet mixture and mix until well combined.
4. Pour the batter into the silicone muffin moulds.
5. Insert a crisper plate in the Ninja Foodi air fryer baskets.
6. Place muffin moulds in both baskets.
7. Select zone 1 then select "bake" mode and set the temperature to 390 degrees F for 17 minutes. Press "start/stop" to begin.

Nutrition Info:

- (Per serving) Calories 173 | Fat 5.8g |Sodium 177mg | Carbs 26.6g | Fiber 2.1g | Sugar 8.7g | Protein 4.2g

Banana And Raisins Muffins

Servings:2 | Cooking Time:16

Ingredients:

- Salt, pinch
- 2 eggs, whisked
- 1/3 cup butter, melted
- 4 tablespoons of almond milk
- ¼ teaspoon of vanilla extract
- ½ teaspoon of baking powder
- 1-1/2 cup all-purpose flour
- 1 cup mashed bananas
- 2 tablespoons of raisins

Directions:

1. Take about 4 large (one-cup sized) ramekins and layer them with muffin papers.
2. Crack eggs in a large bowl, and whisk it all well and start adding vanilla extract, almond milk, baking powder, and melted butter
3. Whisk the ingredients very well.
4. Take a separate bowl and add the all-purpose flour, and salt.
5. Now, combine the add dry ingredients with the wet ingredients.
6. Now, pour mashed bananas and raisins into this batter
7. Mix it well to make a batter for the muffins.
8. Now pour the batter into four ramekins and divided the ramekins in the air fryer zones.
9. Set the timer for zone 1 to 16 minutes at 350 degrees F.
10. Select the MATCH button for the zone 2 basket.
11. Check if not done, and let it AIR FRY for one more minute.
12. Once it is done, serve.

Nutrition Info:

- (Per serving) Calories 727| Fat 43.1g| Sodium366 mg | Carbs 74.4g | Fiber 4.7g | Sugar 16.1g | Protein 14.1g

Sweet Potato Hash

Servings: 4 | Cooking Time: 15 Minutes

Ingredients:

- 3 sweet potatoes, peel & cut into ½-inch pieces
- ½ tsp cinnamon
- 2 tbsp olive oil
- 1 bell pepper, cut into ½-inch pieces
- ½ tsp dried thyme
- ½ tsp nutmeg
- 1 medium onion, cut into ½-inch pieces
- Pepper
- Salt

Directions:

1. In a bowl, toss sweet potatoes with the remaining ingredients.
2. Insert a crisper plate in Ninja Foodi air fryer baskets.
3. Add potato mixture in both baskets.
4. Select zone 1 then select "air fry" mode and set the temperature to 355 degrees F for 15 minutes. Press "match" to match zone 2 settings to zone 1. Press "start/stop" to begin.

Nutrition Info:

- (Per serving) Calories 167 | Fat 7.3g |Sodium 94mg | Carbs 24.9g | Fiber 4.2g | Sugar 6.8g | Protein 2.2g

Pepper Egg Cups

Servings: 4 | Cooking Time: 18 Minutes.

Ingredients:

- 2 halved bell pepper, seeds removed
- 4 eggs
- 1 teaspoon olive oil
- 1 pinch salt and black pepper
- 1 pinch sriracha flakes

Directions:

1. Slice the bell peppers in half, lengthwise, and remove their seeds and the inner portion to get a cup-like shape.
2. Rub olive oil on the edges of the bell peppers.
3. Place them in the two crisper plates with their cut side up and crack 1 egg in each half of bell pepper.
4. Drizzle salt, black pepper, and sriracha flakes on top of the eggs.
5. Return the crisper plates to the Ninja Foodi Dual Zone Air Fryer.
6. Choose the Air Fry mode for Zone 1 and set the temperature to 390 degrees F and the time to 18 minutes.
7. Select the "MATCH" button to copy the settings for Zone 2.
8. Initiate cooking by pressing the START/STOP button.
9. Serve warm and fresh.

Nutrition Info:

- (Per serving) Calories 183 | Fat 15g |Sodium 402mg | Carbs 2.5g | Fiber 0.4g | Sugar 1.1g | Protein 10g

Air Fryer Sausage Patties

Servings: 12 | Cooking Time: 10 Minutes

Ingredients:

- 1-pound pork sausage or ready-made patties
- Fennel seeds or preferred seasonings

Directions:

1. Prepare the sausage by slicing it into patties, then flavor it with fennel seed or your favorite seasonings.
2. Install a crisper plate in both drawers. Place half the patties in zone 1 and half in zone 2, then insert the drawers into the unit.
3. Select zone 1, select AIR FRY, set temperature to 390 degrees F/ 200 degrees C, and set time to 10 minutes.

4. Select MATCH to match zone 2 settings to zone 1.
5. Press the START/STOP button to begin cooking.
6. When cooking is complete, remove the patties from the unit and serve with sauce or make a burger.

Nutrition Info:

• (Per serving) Calories 130 | Fat 10.5g | Sodium 284mg | Carbs 0.3g | Fiber 0.2g | Sugar 0g | Protein 7.4g

Honey Banana Oatmeal

Servings: 4 | Cooking Time: 8 Minutes

Ingredients:

- 2 eggs
- 2 tbsp honey
- 1 tsp vanilla
- 45g quick oats
- 73ml milk
- 30g Greek yoghurt
- 219g banana, mashed

Directions:

1. In a bowl, mix eggs, milk, yoghurt, honey, vanilla, oats, and mashed banana until well combined.
2. Pour batter into the four greased ramekins.
3. Insert a crisper plate in the Ninja Foodi air fryer baskets.
4. Place ramekins in both baskets.
5. Select zone 1 then select "air fry" mode and set the temperature to 390 degrees F for 8 minutes. Press "match" to match zone 2 settings to zone 1. Press "start/stop" to begin.

Nutrition Info:

• (Per serving) Calories 228 | Fat 4.6g |Sodium 42mg | Carbs 40.4g | Fiber 4.2g | Sugar 16.1g | Protein 7.7g

Hash Browns

Servings: 4 | Cooking Time: 5 Minutes

Ingredients:

- 4 frozen hash browns patties
- Cooking oil spray of choice

Directions:

1. Install a crisper plate in both drawers. Place half the hash browns in zone 1 and half in zone 2, then insert the drawers into the unit. Spray the hash browns with some cooking oil.
2. Select zone 1, select AIR FRY, set temperature to 390 degrees F/ 200 degrees C, and set time to 5 minutes.
3. Select MATCH to match zone 2 settings to zone 1. Press the START/STOP button to begin cooking.
4. When cooking is complete, remove the hash browns and serve.

Nutrition Info:

• (Per serving) Calories 130 | Fat 7g | Sodium 300mg | Carbs 15g | Fiber 2g | Sugar 0g | Protein 1g

Donuts

Servings: 6 | Cooking Time: 15 Minutes

Ingredients:

- 1 cup granulated sugar
- 2 tablespoons ground cinnamon
- 1 can refrigerated flaky buttermilk biscuits
- ¼ cup unsalted butter, melted

Directions:

1. Combine the sugar and cinnamon in a small shallow bowl and set aside.
2. Remove the biscuits from the can and put them on a chopping board, separated. Cut holes in the center of each biscuit with a 1-inch round biscuit cutter (or a similarly sized bottle cap).
3. Place a crisper plate in each drawer. In each drawer, place 4 biscuits in a single layer. Insert the drawers into the unit.
4. Select zone 1, then AIR FRY, then set the temperature to 360 degrees F/ 180 degrees C with a 10-minute timer. To match zone 2 settings to zone 1, choose MATCH. To begin cooking, select START/STOP.
5. Remove the donuts from the drawers after the timer has finished.

Nutrition Info:

• (Per serving) Calories 223 | Fat 8g | Sodium 150mg | Carbs 40g | Fiber 1.4g | Sugar 34.2g | Protein 0.8g

Bagels

Servings: 8 | Cooking Time: 15 Minutes

Ingredients:

- 2 cups self-rising flour
- 2 cups non-fat plain Greek yogurt
- 2 beaten eggs for egg wash (optional)
- ½ cup sesame seeds (optional)

Directions:

1. In a medium mixing bowl, combine the self-rising flour and Greek yogurt using a wooden spoon.
2. Knead the dough for about 5 minutes on a lightly floured board.
3. Divide the dough into four equal pieces and roll each into a thin rope, securing the ends to form a bagel shape.
4. Install a crisper plate in both drawers. Place 4 bagels in a single layer in each drawer. Insert the drawers into the unit.
5. Select zone 1, select AIR FRY, set temperature to 360 degrees F/ 180 degrees C, and set time to 15 minutes. Select MATCH to match zone 2 settings to zone 1. Select START/STOP to begin.
6. Once the timer has finished, remove the bagels from

the units.
7. Serve and enjoy!

Nutrition Info:

- (Per serving) Calories 202 | Fat 4.5g | Sodium 55mg | Carbs 31.3g | Fiber 2.7g | Sugar 4.7g | Protein 8.7g

Breakfast Stuffed Peppers

Servings: 4 | Cooking Time: 13 Minutes

Ingredients:

- 2 capsicums, halved, seeds removed
- 4 eggs
- 1 teaspoon olive oil
- 1 pinch salt and pepper
- 1 pinch sriracha flakes

Directions:

1. Cut each capsicum in half and place two halves in each air fryer basket.
2. Crack one egg into each capsicum and top it with black pepper, salt, sriracha flakes and olive oil.
3. Return the air fryer basket 1 to Zone 1, and basket 2 to Zone 2 of the Ninja Foodi 2-Basket Air Fryer.
4. Choose the "Air Fry" mode for Zone 1 at 390 degrees F and 13 minutes of cooking time.
5. Select the "MATCH COOK" option to copy the settings for Zone 2.
6. Initiate cooking by pressing the START/PAUSE BUTTON.
7. Serve warm.

Nutrition Info:

- (Per serving) Calories 237 | Fat 19g |Sodium 518mg | Carbs 7g | Fiber 1.5g | Sugar 3.4g | Protein 12g

Cinnamon-raisin Bagels Everything Bagels

Servings:4 | Cooking Time: 14 Minutes

Ingredients:

- FOR THE BAGEL DOUGH
- 1 cup all-purpose flour, plus more for dusting
- 2 teaspoons baking powder
- 1 teaspoon kosher salt
- 1 cup reduced-fat plain Greek yogurt
- FOR THE CINNAMON-RAISIN BAGELS
- ¼ cup raisins
- ½ teaspoon ground cinnamon
- FOR THE EVERYTHING BAGELS
- ¼ teaspoon poppy seeds
- ¼ teaspoon sesame seeds
- ¼ teaspoon dried minced garlic
- ¼ teaspoon dried minced onion
- FOR THE EGG WASH
- 1 large egg
- 1 tablespoon water

Directions:

1. To prep the bagels: In a large bowl, combine the flour, baking powder, and salt. Stir in the yogurt to form a soft dough. Turn the dough out onto a lightly floured surface and knead five to six times, until it is smooth and elastic. Divide the dough in half.
2. Knead the raisins and cinnamon into one dough half. Leave the other dough half plain.
3. Divide both portions of dough in half to form a total of 4 balls of dough (2 cinnamon-raisin and 2 plain). Roll each ball of dough into a rope about 8 inches long. Shape each rope into a ring and pinch the ends to seal.
4. To prep the everything bagels: In a small bowl, mix together the poppy seeds, sesame seeds, garlic, and onion.
5. To prep the egg wash: In a second small bowl, beat together the egg and water. Brush the egg wash on top of each bagel.
6. Generously sprinkle the everything seasoning over the top of the 2 plain bagels.
7. To cook the bagels: Install a crisper plate in each of the two baskets. Place the cinnamon-raisin bagels in the Zone 1 basket and insert the basket in the unit. For best results, the bagels should not overlap in the basket. Place the everything bagels in the Zone 2 basket and insert the basket in the unit.
8. Select Zone 1, select AIR FRY, set the temperature to 325°F, and set the time to 14 minutes. Select MATCH COOK to match Zone 2 settings to Zone 1.
9. Press START/PAUSE to begin cooking.
10. When cooking is complete, use silicone-tipped tongs to transfer the bagels to a cutting board. Let cool for 2 to 3 minutes before cutting and serving.

Nutrition Info:

- (Per serving) Calories: 238; Total fat: 3g; Saturated fat: 1g; Carbohydrates: 43g; Fiber: 1.5g; Protein: 11g; Sodium: 321mg

Poultry Recipes

Balsamic Duck Breast

Servings: 2 | Cooking Time: 20 Minutes.

Ingredients:

- 2 duck breasts
- 1 teaspoon parsley
- Salt and black pepper, to taste
- Marinade:
- 1 tablespoon olive oil
- ½ teaspoon French mustard
- 1 teaspoon dried garlic
- 2 teaspoons honey
- ½ teaspoon balsamic vinegar

Directions:

1. Mix olive oil, mustard, garlic, honey, and balsamic vinegar in a bowl.
2. Add duck breasts to the marinade and rub well.
3. Place one duck breast in each crisper plate.
4. Return the crisper plates to the Ninja Foodi Dual Zone Air Fryer.
5. Choose the Air Fry mode for Zone 1 and set the temperature to 360 degrees F and the time to 20 minutes.
6. Select the "MATCH" button to copy the settings for Zone 2.
7. Initiate cooking by pressing the START/STOP button.
8. Flip the duck breasts once cooked halfway through, then resume cooking.
9. Serve warm.

Nutrition Info:

- (Per serving) Calories 546 | Fat 33.1g |Sodium 1201mg | Carbs 30g | Fiber 2.4g | Sugar 9.7g | Protein 32g

Crispy Fried Quail

Servings: 8 | Cooking Time: 6 Minutes

Ingredients:

- 8 boneless quail breasts
- 2 tablespoons Sichuan pepper dry rub mix
- ¾ cup rice flour
- ¼ cup all-purpose flour
- 2-3 cups peanut oil
- Garnish
- Sliced jalapenos
- Fresh lime wedges
- Fresh coriander

Directions:

1. Split the quail breasts in half.
2. Mix Sichuan mix with flours in a bowl.
3. Coat the quail breasts with flour mixture and place in the air fryer baskets.
4. Return the air fryer basket 1 to Zone 1, and basket 2 to Zone 2 of the Ninja Foodi 2-Basket Air Fryer.
5. Choose the "Air Fry" mode for Zone 1 at 300 degrees F and 6 minutes of cooking time.
6. Select the "MATCH COOK" option to copy the settings for Zone 2.
7. Initiate cooking by pressing the START/PAUSE BUTTON.
8. Flip the quail breasts once cooked halfway through.
9. Serve warm.

Nutrition Info:

- (Per serving) Calories 351 | Fat 11g |Sodium 150mg | Carbs 3.3g | Fiber 0.2g | Sugar 1g | Protein 33.2g

Chicken And Broccoli

Servings: 4 | Cooking Time: 15 Minutes

Ingredients:

- 1-pound boneless, skinless chicken breast or thighs, cut into 1-inch bite-sized pieces
- ¼ –½ pound broccoli, cut into florets (1–2 cups)
- ½ medium onion, cut into thick slices
- 3 tablespoons olive oil or grape seed oil
- ½ teaspoon garlic powder
- 1 tablespoon fresh minced ginger
- 1 tablespoon low-sodium soy sauce
- 1 tablespoon rice vinegar
- 1 teaspoon sesame oil
- 2 teaspoons hot sauce (optional)
- ½ teaspoon sea salt, or to taste
- Black pepper, to taste
- Lemon wedges, for serving (optional)

Directions:

1. Combine the oil, garlic powder, ginger, soy sauce, rice vinegar, sesame oil, optional spicy sauce, salt, and pepper in a large mixing bowl.
2. Put the chicken in a separate bowl.
3. In a separate bowl, combine the broccoli and onions.
4. Divide the marinade between the two bowls and toss to evenly coat each.
5. Install a crisper plate into both drawers. Place the broccoli in the zone 1 drawer, then insert the drawer into the unit. Place the chicken breasts in the zone 2 drawer, then insert the drawer into the unit.
6. Select zone 1, select AIR FRY, set temperature to 390 degrees F/ 200 degrees C, and set time to 10 minutes. Select zone 2, select AIR FRY, set temperature to 390 degrees F/ 200 degrees C, and set time to 20 minutes. Select SYNC. Press the START/STOP button to begin cooking.
7. When zone 2 time reaches 9 minutes, press START/STOP to pause the unit. Remove the drawer and toss the chicken. Re-insert the drawer into the unit and press START/STOP to resume cooking.
8. When cooking is complete, serve the chicken breasts and broccoli while still hot.
9. Add additional salt and pepper to taste. Squeeze optional fresh lemon juice on top and serve warm.

Nutrition Info:

- (Per serving) Calories 224 | Fat 15.8g | Sodium 203mg | Carbs 4g | Fiber 1g | Sugar 1g | Protein 25g

Thai Chicken Meatballs

Servings: 4 | Cooking Time: 10 Minutes

Ingredients:

- ½ cup sweet chili sauce
- 2 tablespoons lime juice
- 2 tablespoons ketchup
- 1 teaspoon soy sauce
- 1 large egg, lightly beaten
- ¾ cup panko breadcrumbs
- 1 green onion, finely chopped
- 1 tablespoon minced fresh cilantro
- ½ teaspoon salt
- ½ teaspoon garlic powder
- 1-pound lean ground chicken

Directions:

1. Combine the chili sauce, lime juice, ketchup, and soy sauce in a small bowl; set aside ½ cup for serving.
2. Combine the egg, breadcrumbs, green onion, cilantro, salt, garlic powder, and the remaining 4 tablespoons chili sauce mixture in a large mixing bowl. Mix in the chicken lightly yet thoroughly. Form into 12 balls.
3. Install a crisper plate in both drawers. Place half the chicken meatballs in the zone 1 drawer and half in zone 2's, then insert the drawers into the unit.
4. Select zone 1, select AIR FRY, set temperature to 390 degrees F/ 200 degrees C, and set time to 10 minutes. Select MATCH to match zone 2 settings to zone 1. Press the START/STOP button to begin cooking.
5. When the time reaches 5 minutes, press START/STOP to pause the unit. Remove the drawers and flip the chicken. Re-insert the drawers into the unit and press START/STOP to resume cooking.
6. When cooking is complete, remove the chicken meatballs and serve hot.

Nutrition Info:

- (Per serving) Calories 93 | Fat 3g | Sodium 369mg | Carbs 9g | Fiber 0g | Sugar 6g | Protein 9g

Honey Butter Chicken

Servings: 4 | Cooking Time: 15 Minutes

Ingredients:

- 4 chicken breasts, boneless
- 85g honey
- 28g butter, melted
- 2 tsp lemon juice
- 15ml olive oil
- 62g Dijon mustard
- Pepper
- Salt

Directions:

1. In a small bowl, mix butter, oil, lemon juice, honey, mustard, pepper, and salt.
2. Insert a crisper plate in the Ninja Foodi air fryer baskets.
3. Brush chicken breasts with butter mixture and place them in both baskets.
4. Select zone 1 then select "bake" mode and set the temperature to 380 degrees F for 15 minutes. Press "match" to match zone 2 settings to zone 1. Press "start/stop" to begin.

Nutrition Info:

- (Per serving) Calories 434 | Fat 20.7g |Sodium 384mg | Carbs 18.4g | Fiber 0.6g | Sugar 17.6g | Protein 43.1g

Cheddar-stuffed Chicken

Servings: 4 | Cooking Time: 20 Minutes.

Ingredients:

- 3 bacon strips, cooked and crumbled
- 2 ounces Cheddar cheese, cubed
- ¼ cup barbeque sauce
- 2 (4 ounces) boneless chicken breasts
- Salt and black pepper to taste

Directions:

1. Make a 1-inch deep pouch in each chicken breast.
2. Mix cheddar cubes with half of the BBQ sauce, salt, black pepper, and bacon.
3. Divide this filling in the chicken breasts and secure the edges with a toothpick.
4. Brush the remaining BBQ sauce over the chicken breasts.
5. Place the chicken in the crisper plate and spray them with cooking oil.
6. Return the crisper plate to the Ninja Foodi Dual Zone Air Fryer.
7. Choose the Air Fry mode for Zone 1 and set the temperature to 360 degrees F and the time to 20 minutes.
8. Initiate cooking by pressing the START/STOP button.
9. Serve warm.

Nutrition Info:

- (Per serving) Calories 379 | Fat 19g |Sodium 184mg | Carbs 12.3g | Fiber 0.6g | Sugar 2g | Protein 37.7g

Chicken Breast Strips

Servings:2 | Cooking Time:22

Ingredients:

- 2 large organic egg
- 1-ounce buttermilk
- 1 cup of cornmeal
- ¼ cup all-purpose flour
- Salt and black pepper, to taste
- 1 pound of chicken breasts, cut into strips
- 2 tablespoons of oil bay seasoning
- oil spray, for greasing

Directions:

1. Take a medium bowl and whisk eggs with buttermilk.
2. In a separate large bowl mix flour, cornmeal, salt, black pepper, and oil bay seasoning.
3. First, dip the chicken breast strip in egg wash and then dredge into the flour mixture.
4. Coat the strip all over and layer on both the baskets that are already grease with oil spray.
5. Grease the chicken breast strips with oil spray as well.
6. Set the zone 1 basket to AIR FRY mode at 400 degrees F for 22 minutes.
7. Select the MATCH button for zone 2.
8. Hit the start button to let the cooking start.
9. Once the cooking cycle is done, serve.

Nutrition Info:

- (Per serving) Calories 788| Fat25g| Sodium835 mg | Carbs60g | Fiber 4.9g| Sugar1.5g | Protein79g

Turkey Burger Patties

Servings: 4 | Cooking Time: 14 Minutes

Ingredients:

- 1 egg white
- 453g ground turkey
- 30ml Worcestershire sauce
- ½ tsp dried basil
- ½ tsp dried oregano
- Pepper
- Salt

Directions:

1. In a bowl, mix ground turkey with remaining ingredients until well combined.
2. Insert a crisper plate in the Ninja Foodi air fryer baskets.
3. Make patties from the turkey mixture and place them in both baskets.
4. Select zone 1, then select "air fry" mode and set the temperature to 360 degrees F for 14 minutes. Press

"match" to match zone 2 settings to zone 1. Press "start/stop" to begin.

Nutrition Info:

- (Per serving) Calories 234 | Fat 12.5g |Sodium 251mg | Carbs 1.7g | Fiber 0.1g | Sugar 1.6g | Protein 32g

Chicken Drumsticks

Servings: 6 | Cooking Time: 15 Minutes

Ingredients:

- 12 chicken drumsticks
- 72g chilli garlic sauce
- 2 tbsp ginger, minced
- 1 tbsp garlic, minced
- 3 green onion stalks, chopped
- 60ml orange juice
- 60ml soy sauce
- ½ medium onion, sliced
- Pepper
- Salt

Directions:

1. Add all the ingredients except the drumsticks into a blender and blend until smooth.
2. Place the chicken drumsticks in bowl.
3. Pour the blended mixture over chicken drumsticks and mix well.
4. Cover the bowl and place in refrigerator for 1 hour.
5. Insert a crisper plate in the Ninja Foodi air fryer baskets.
6. Place the marinated chicken drumsticks in both baskets.
7. Select zone 1 then select "air fry" mode and set the temperature to 390 degrees F for 15 minutes. Press "match" and then"start/stop" to begin.

Nutrition Info:

- (Per serving) Calories 178 | Fat 5.4g |Sodium 701mg | Carbs 4.5g | Fiber 0.6g | Sugar 1.5g | Protein 26.4g

Lemon Chicken Thighs

Servings: 4 | Cooking Time: 25 Minutes

Ingredients:

- ¼ cup butter, softened
- 3 garlic cloves, minced
- 2 teaspoons minced fresh rosemary or ½ teaspoon crushed dried rosemary
- 1 teaspoon minced fresh thyme or ¼ teaspoon dried thyme
- 1 teaspoon grated lemon zest
- 1 tablespoon lemon juice
- 4 bone-in chicken thighs (about 1½ pounds)
- 1⁄8 teaspoon salt
- 1⁄8 teaspoon pepper

Directions:

1. Combine the butter, garlic, rosemary, thyme, lemon zest, and lemon juice in a small bowl.
2. Under the skin of each chicken thigh, spread 1 teaspoon of the butter mixture. Apply the remaining butter to each thigh's skin. Season to taste with salt and pepper.
3. Install a crisper plate in both drawers. Place half the chicken tenders in the zone 1 drawer and half in zone 2's, then insert the drawers into the unit.
4. Select zone 1, select AIR FRY, set temperature to 390 degrees F/ 200 degrees C, and set time to 22 minutes. Select MATCH to match zone 2 settings to zone 1. Press the START/STOP button to begin cooking.
5. When the time reaches 11 minutes, press START/STOP to pause the unit. Remove the drawers and flip the chicken. Re-insert the drawers into the unit and press START/STOP to resume cooking.
6. When cooking is complete, remove the chicken and serve.

Nutrition Info:

- (Per serving) Calories 329 | Fat 26g | Sodium 253mg | Carbs 1g | Fiber 0g | Sugar 0g | Protein 23g

"fried" Chicken With Warm Baked Potato Salad

Servings:4 | Cooking Time: 40 Minutes

Ingredients:

- FOR THE "FRIED" CHICKEN
- 1 cup buttermilk
- 1 tablespoon kosher salt
- 4 bone-in, skin-on chicken drumsticks and/or thighs
- 2 cups all-purpose flour
- 1 tablespoon seasoned salt
- 1 tablespoon paprika
- Nonstick cooking spray
- FOR THE POTATO SALAD
- 1½ pounds baby red potatoes, halved
- 1 tablespoon vegetable oil
- ½ cup mayonnaise
- ⅓ cup plain reduced-fat Greek yogurt
- 1 tablespoon apple cider vinegar
- ½ teaspoon kosher salt
- ½ teaspoon freshly ground black pepper
- ¾ cup shredded Cheddar cheese
- 4 slices cooked bacon, crumbled
- 3 scallions, sliced

Directions:

1. To prep the chicken: In a large bowl, combine the buttermilk and salt. Add the chicken and turn to coat. Let rest for at least 30 minutes (for the best flavor, marinate the chicken overnight in the refrigerator).

2. In a separate large bowl, combine the flour, seasoned salt, and paprika.
3. Remove the chicken from the marinade and allow any excess marinade to drip off. Discard the marinade. Dip the chicken pieces in the flour, coating them thoroughly. Mist with cooking spray. Let the chicken rest for 10 minutes.
4. To prep the potatoes: In a large bowl, combine the potatoes and oil and toss to coat.
5. To cook the chicken and potatoes: Install a crisper plate in the Zone 1 basket. Place the chicken in the basket in a single layer and insert the basket in the unit. Place the potatoes in the Zone 2 basket and insert the basket in the unit.
6. Select Zone 1, select AIR FRY, set the temperature to 390°F, and set the time to 30 minutes.
7. Select Zone 2, select BAKE, set the temperature to 400°F, and set the time to 40 minutes. Select SMART FINISH.
8. Press START/PAUSE to begin cooking.
9. When cooking is complete, the chicken will be golden brown and cooked through (an instant-read thermometer should read 165°F) and the potatoes will be fork-tender.
10. Rinse the potatoes under cold water for about 1 minute to cool them.
11. Place the potatoes in a large bowl and stir in the mayonnaise, yogurt, vinegar, salt, and black pepper. Gently stir in the Cheddar, bacon, and scallions. Serve warm with the "fried" chicken.

Nutrition Info:

• (Per serving) Calories: 639; Total fat: 38g; Saturated fat: 9.5g; Carbohydrates: 54g; Fiber: 4g; Protein: 21g; Sodium: 1,471mg

Chicken Vegetable Skewers

Servings: 6 | Cooking Time: 15 Minutes

Ingredients:

- 900g chicken breasts, cubed
- 1 bell pepper, chopped
- 51g Swerve
- 1 tsp ginger, grated
- 350g zucchini, chopped
- 8 mushrooms, sliced
- ½ medium onion, chopped
- 6 garlic cloves, crushed
- 120ml soy sauce

Directions:

1. Add chicken and the remaining ingredients to a ziplock bag. Seal the bag and place it in the refrigerator overnight.
2. Thread the marinated chicken, zucchini, mushrooms, onion, and bell pepper onto the skewers.
3. Insert a crisper plate in the Ninja Foodi air fryer baskets.
4. Place skewers in both baskets.
5. Select zone 1 then select "air fry" mode and set the temperature to 380 degrees F for 15 minutes. Press "match" to match zone 2 settings to zone 1. Press "start/stop" to begin.

Nutrition Info:

• (Per serving) Calories 329 | Fat 11.5g |Sodium 1335mg | Carbs 8.6g | Fiber 1.4g | Sugar 2.9g | Protein 46.8g

Chicken Wings

Servings:3 | Cooking Time:20

Ingredients:

- 1 cup chicken batter mix, Louisiana
- 9 Chicken wings
- ½ teaspoon of smoked paprika
- 2 tablespoons of Dijon mustard
- 1 tablespoon of cayenne pepper
- 1 teaspoon of meat tenderizer, powder
- oil spray, for greasing

Directions:

1. Pat dry chicken wings and add mustard, paprika, meat tenderizer, and cayenne pepper.
2. Dredge it in the chicken batter mix.
3. Oil sprays the chicken wings.
4. Grease both baskets of the air fryer.
5. Divide the wings between the two zones of the air fryer.
6. Set zone 1 to AR FRY mode at 400 degrees F for 20 minutes
7. Select MATCH for zone 2.
8. Hit start to begin with the cooking.
9. Once the cooking cycle complete, serve, and enjoy hot.

Nutrition Info:

• (Per serving) Calories621 | Fat 32.6g| Sodium 2016mg | Carbs 46.6g | Fiber 1.1g | Sugar 0.2g | Protein 32.1g

Italian Chicken & Potatoes

Servings: 4 | Cooking Time: 24 Minutes

Ingredients:

- 450g chicken breast, boneless & diced
- 30ml olive oil
- ½ tsp lemon zest
- 2 tbsp fresh lemon juice
- 450g baby potatoes, quartered
- 1 tbsp Greek seasoning
- Pepper
- Salt

Directions:

1. Toss potatoes with ½ tablespoon Greek seasoning, 1 tablespoon oil, lemon zest, lemon juice, pepper, and salt in a bowl.
2. Insert a crisper plate in the Ninja Foodi air fryer baskets.
3. Add potatoes into the zone 1 basket.
4. In a bowl, toss chicken with the remaining oil and seasoning.
5. Add the chicken into the zone 2 basket.
6. Select zone 1, then select "air fry" mode and set the temperature to 390 degrees F for 12 minutes. Press "match" to match zone 2 settings to zone 1. Press "start/stop" to begin.

Nutrition Info:

• (Per serving) Calories 262 | Fat 10.1g |Sodium 227mg | Carbs 15.5g | Fiber 2.9g | Sugar 0.2g | Protein 27.2g

Spicy Chicken Wings

Servings: 8 | Cooking Time: 30 Minutes

Ingredients:

- 900g chicken wings
- 1 tsp black pepper
- 12g brown sugar
- 1 tbsp chilli powder
- 57g butter, melted
- 1 tsp smoked paprika
- 1 tsp garlic powder
- 1 tsp salt

Directions:

1. In a bowl, toss chicken wings with remaining ingredients until well coated.
2. Insert a crisper plate in the Ninja Foodi air fryer baskets.
3. Add the chicken wings to both baskets.
4. Select zone 1, then select "air fry" mode and set the temperature to 355 degrees F for 30 minutes. Press "match" to match zone 2 settings to zone 1. Press "start/stop" to begin. Turn halfway through.

Nutrition Info:

• (Per serving) Calories 276 | Fat 14.4g |Sodium 439mg | Carbs 2.2g | Fiber 0.5g | Sugar 1.3g | Protein 33.1g

Cornish Hen With Asparagus

Servings:2 | Cooking Time:45

Ingredients:

- 10 spears of asparagus
- Salt and black pepper, to taste
- 1 Cornish hen
- Salt, to taste
- Black pepper, to taste
- 1 teaspoon of Paprika
- Coconut spray, for greasing
- 2 lemons, sliced

Directions:

1. Wash and pat dry the asparagus and coat it with coconut oil spray.
2. Sprinkle salt on the asparagus and place inside the first basket of the air fryer.
3. Next, take the Cornish hen and rub it well with the salt, black pepper, and paprika.
4. Oil sprays the Cornish hen and place in the second air fryer basket.
5. Press button 1 for the first basket and set it to AIR FRY mode at 350 degrees F, for 8 minutes.
6. For the second basket hit 2 and set the time to 45 minutes at 350 degrees F, by selecting the ROAST mode.
7. To start cooking, hit the smart finish button and press hit start.
8. Once the 6 minutes pass press 1 and pause and take out the asparagus.
9. Once the chicken cooking cycle complete, press 2 and hit pause.
10. Take out the Basket of chicken and let it transfer to the serving plate
11. Serve the chicken with roasted asparagus and slices of lemon.
12. Serve hot and enjoy.

Nutrition Info:

• (Per serving) Calories 192| Fat 4.7g| Sodium 151mg | Carbs10.7 g | Fiber 4.6g | Sugar 3.8g | Protein 30g

Teriyaki Chicken Skewers

Servings: 4 | Cooking Time: 16 Minutes

Ingredients:

- 455g boneless chicken thighs, cubed
- 237ml teriyaki marinade
- 16 small wooden skewers
- Sesame seeds for rolling
- Teriyaki Marinade
- ⅓ cup soy sauce
- 59ml chicken broth
- ½ orange, juiced
- 2 tablespoons brown sugar
- 1 teaspoon ginger, grated
- 1 clove garlic, grated

Directions:

1. Blend teriyaki marinade ingredients in a blender.
2. Add chicken and its marinade to a Ziplock bag.
3. Seal this bag, shake it well and refrigerate for 30 minutes.
4. Thread the chicken on the wooden skewers.
5. Place these skewers in the air fryer baskets.
6. Return the air fryer basket 1 to Zone 1, and basket 2

to Zone 2 of the Ninja Foodi 2-Basket Air Fryer.
7. Choose the "Air Fry" mode for Zone 1 at 350 degrees F and 16 minutes of cooking time.
8. Select the "MATCH COOK" option to copy the settings for Zone 2.
9. Initiate cooking by pressing the START/PAUSE BUTTON.
10. Flip the skewers once cooked halfway through.
11. Garnish with sesame seeds.
12. Serve warm.

Nutrition Info:

- (Per serving) Calories 456 | Fat 16.4g |Sodium 1321mg | Carbs 19.2g | Fiber 2.2g | Sugar 4.2g | Protein 55.2g

Chicken Potatoes

Servings: 4 | Cooking Time: 22 Minutes.

Ingredients:

- 15 ounces canned potatoes drained
- 1 teaspoon olive oil
- 1 teaspoon Lawry's seasoned salt
- ⅛ teaspoons black pepper optional
- 8 ounces boneless chicken breast cubed
- ¼ teaspoon paprika
- ⅜ cup cheddar, shredded
- 4 bacon slices, cooked, cut into strips

Directions:

1. Dice the chicken into small pieces and toss them with olive oil and spices.
2. Drain and dice the potato pieces into smaller cubes.
3. Add potato to the chicken and mix well to coat.
4. Spread the mixture in the two crisper plates in a single layer.
5. Return the crisper plates to the Ninja Foodi Dual Zone Air Fryer.
6. Choose the Air Fry mode for Zone 1 and set the temperature to 390 degrees F and the time to 22 minutes.
7. Select the "MATCH" button to copy the settings for Zone 2.
8. Initiate cooking by pressing the START/STOP button.
9. Top the chicken and potatoes with cheese and bacon.
10. Return the crisper plates to the Ninja Foodi Dual Zone Air Fryer.
11. Select the Max Crisp mode for Zone 1 and set the temperature to 300 degrees F and the time to 5 minutes.
12. Initiate cooking by pressing the START/STOP button.
13. Repeat the same step for Zone 2 to broil the potatoes and chicken in the right drawer.
14. Enjoy with dried herbs on top.

Nutrition Info:

- (Per serving) Calories 346 | Fat 16.1g |Sodium 882mg | Carbs 1.3g | Fiber 0.5g | Sugar 0.5g | Protein 48.2g

Chicken Parmesan With Roasted Lemon-parmesan Broccoli

Servings:4 | Cooking Time: 18 Minutes

Ingredients:

- FOR THE CHICKEN PARMESAN
- 2 tablespoons all-purpose flour
- 2 large eggs
- 1 cup panko bread crumbs
- 2 tablespoons grated Parmesan cheese
- 2 teaspoons Italian seasoning
- 4 thin-sliced chicken cutlets (4 ounces each)
- 2 tablespoons vegetable oil
- ½ cup marinara sauce
- ½ cup shredded part-skim mozzarella cheese
- FOR THE BROCCOLI
- 4 cups broccoli florets
- 2 tablespoons olive oil, divided
- ¼ teaspoon kosher salt
- ¼ teaspoon freshly ground black pepper
- 2 teaspoons fresh lemon juice
- 2 tablespoons grated Parmesan cheese

Directions:

1. To prep the chicken Parmesan: Set up a breading station with 3 small shallow bowls. Place the flour in the first bowl. In the second bowl, beat the eggs. Combine the panko, Parmesan, and Italian seasoning in the third bowl.
2. Bread the chicken cutlets in this order: First, dip them into the flour, coating both sides. Then, dip into the beaten egg. Finally, place in the panko mixture, coating both sides of the cutlets. Drizzle the oil over the cutlets.
3. To prep the broccoli: In a large bowl, combine the broccoli, 1 tablespoon of olive oil, the salt, and black pepper.
4. To cook the chicken and broccoli: Install a crisper plate in the Zone 1 basket. Place the chicken in the basket and insert the basket in the unit. Place the broccoli in the Zone 2 basket and insert the basket in the unit.
5. Select Zone 1, select AIR FRY, set the temperature to 390°F, and set the time to 18 minutes.
6. Select Zone 2, select ROAST, set the temperature to 390°F, and set the time to 15 minutes. Select SMART FINISH.
7. Press START/PAUSE to begin cooking.
8. When the Zone 1 timer reads 10 minutes, press START/PAUSE. Remove the basket and use silicone-tipped tongs to flip the chicken. Reinsert the basket and press START/PAUSE to resume cooking.
9. When the Zone 1 timer reads 2 minutes, press START/PAUSE. Remove the basket and spoon 2 tablespoons of marinara sauce over each chicken cutlet. Sprinkle the

mozzarella on top. Reinsert the basket and press START/PAUSE to resume cooking.

10. When cooking is complete, the cheese will be melted and the chicken cooked through (an instant-read thermometer should read 165°F). Transfer the broccoli to a large bowl. Add the lemon juice and Parmesan and toss to coat. Serve the chicken and broccoli warm.

Nutrition Info:

• (Per serving) Calories: 462; Total fat: 22g; Saturated fat: 5g; Carbohydrates: 25g; Fiber: 2.5g; Protein: 37g; Sodium: 838mg

Jamaican Fried Chicken

Servings: 6 | Cooking Time: 25 Minutes

Ingredients:

- 6-8 chicken thighs
- Egg Marinade:
- 2 teaspoons of hot sauce
- 1 teaspoon of ground ginger
- 1 teaspoon of ground onion
- 1 teaspoon of black pepper
- 1 teaspoon of ground garlic
- 237ml of almond milk
- 1 tablespoon of lemon juice
- 1 large egg
- Breading:
- 2 cups of ground almonds
- ⅓ cup of tapioca starch
- 1 tablespoon of paprika
- 1 tablespoon of thyme
- 1 tablespoon of parsley
- 1 teaspoon of garlic powder
- 1 teaspoon of onion powder
- ½ teaspoon of cayenne pepper
- 1 teaspoon of pink salt
- Spray on cooking oil olive oil spray

Directions:

1. Mix egg marinade ingredients in a large bowl and add chicken thighs.
2. Stir well to coat then cover and refrigerate for 30 minutes.
3. Meanwhile, mix all the breading ingredients in a shallow bowl.
4. Remove the chicken from the egg marinade and coat with the breading mixture.
5. Place the coated chicken thighs in the air fryer baskets.
6. Return the air fryer basket 1 to Zone 1, and basket 2 to Zone 2 of the Ninja Foodi 2-Basket Air Fryer.
7. Choose the "Air Fry" mode for Zone 1 and set the temperature to 375 degrees F and 25 minutes of cooking time.
8. Select the "MATCH COOK" option to copy the settings for Zone 2.
9. Initiate cooking by pressing the START/PAUSE BUTTON.
10. Flip the chicken thighs once cooked halfway through.
11. Serve.

Nutrition Info:

• (Per serving) Calories 268 | Fat 10.4g |Sodium 411mg | Carbs 0.4g | Fiber 0.1g | Sugar 0.1g | Protein 40.6g

Dijon Chicken Wings

Servings: 3 | Cooking Time: 20 Minutes

Ingredients:

- 1 cup chicken batter mix, Louisiana
- 9 chicken wings
- ½ teaspoon smoked Paprika
- 2 tablespoons Dijon mustard
- 1 tablespoon cayenne pepper
- 1 teaspoon meat tenderizer, powder
- Oil spray, for greasing

Directions:

1. Pat dry the chicken wings and add mustard, paprika, meat tenderizer, and cayenne pepper.
2. Dredge the wings in the chicken batter mix.
3. Oil spray the chicken wings.
4. Grease both baskets of the air fryer.
5. Divide the wings between the two zones of the air fryer.
6. Set zone 1 to AIR FRY mode at 400 degrees F/ 200 degrees C for 20 minutes.
7. Select MATCH for zone 2.
8. Hit START/STOP button to begin the cooking.
9. Once the cooking cycle is complete, serve, and enjoy hot.

Nutrition Info:

• (Per serving) Calories 621 | Fat 32.6g | Sodium 2016mg | Carbs 46.6g | Fiber 1.1g | Sugar 0.2g | Protein 32.1g

Chicken Caprese

Servings: 4 | Cooking Time: 10 Minutes

Ingredients:

- 4 chicken breast cutlets
- 1 teaspoon Italian seasoning
- 1 teaspoon salt
- ½ teaspoon black pepper
- 4 slices fresh mozzarella cheese
- 1 large tomato, sliced
- Basil and balsamic vinegar to garnish

Directions:

1. Pat dry the chicken cutlets with a kitchen towel.
2. Rub the chicken with Italian seasoning, black pepper and salt.
3. Place two chicken breasts in each air fryer basket.
4. Return the air fryer basket 1 to Zone 1, and basket 2 to Zone 2 of the Ninja Foodi 2-Basket Air Fryer.
5. Choose the "Air Fry" mode for Zone 1 at 375 degrees F and 10 minutes of cooking time.
6. Select the "MATCH COOK" option to copy the settings for Zone 2.
7. Initiate cooking by pressing the START/PAUSE BUTTON.
8. After 10 minutes top each chicken breast with a slice of cheese and tomato slices.
9. Return the baskets to the Ninja Foodi 2 Baskets Air Fryer and air fry for 5 another minutes.
10. Garnish with balsamic vinegar and basil.
11. Serve warm.

Nutrition Info:

- (Per serving) Calories 502 | Fat 25g |Sodium 230mg | Carbs 1.5g | Fiber 0.2g | Sugar 0.4g | Protein 64.1g

Asian Chicken

Servings: 4 | Cooking Time: 12 Minutes

Ingredients:

- 8 chicken thighs, boneless
- 4 garlic cloves, minced
- 85g honey
- 120ml soy sauce
- 1 tsp dried oregano
- 2 tbsp parsley, chopped
- 1 tbsp ketchup

Directions:

1. Add chicken and remaining ingredients in a bowl and mix until well coated. Cover and place in the refrigerator for 6 hours.
2. Insert a crisper plate in the Ninja Foodi air fryer baskets.
3. Remove the chicken from the marinade and place them in both baskets.
4. Select zone 1 then select "air fry" mode and set the temperature to 390 degrees F for 12 minutes. Press "match" to match zone 2 settings to zone 1. Press "start/stop" to begin.

Nutrition Info:

- (Per serving) Calories 646 | Fat 21.7g |Sodium 2092mg | Carbs 22.2g | Fiber 0.6g | Sugar 18.9g | Protein 86.9g

Chicken Parmesan

Servings: 4 | Cooking Time: 20 Minutes

Ingredients:

- 2 large eggs
- ½ cup seasoned breadcrumbs
- 1/3 cup grated parmesan cheese
- ¼ teaspoon pepper
- 4 boneless, skinless chicken breast halves (6 ounces each)
- 1 cup pasta sauce
- 1 cup shredded mozzarella cheese
- Chopped fresh basil (optional)

Directions:

1. Lightly beat the eggs in a small bowl.
2. Combine the breadcrumbs, parmesan cheese, and pepper in a shallow bowl.
3. After dipping the chicken in the egg, coat it in the crumb mixture.
4. Install a crisper plate in both drawers. Place half the chicken breasts in the zone 1 drawer and half in zone 2's, then insert the drawers into the unit.
5. Select zone 1, select AIR FRY, set temperature to 390 degrees F/ 200 degrees C, and set time to 20 minutes. Select MATCH to match zone 2 settings to zone 1. Press the START/STOP button to begin cooking.
6. When the time reaches 10 minutes, press START/STOP to pause the unit. Remove the drawers and flip the chicken. Re-insert the drawers into the unit and press START/STOP to resume cooking.
7. When cooking is complete, remove the chicken.

Nutrition Info:

- (Per serving) Calories 293 | Fat 15.8g | Sodium 203mg | Carbs 11.1g | Fiber 2.4g | Sugar 8.7g | Protein 29g

Air-fried Turkey Breast With Roasted Green Bean Casserole

Servings:4 | Cooking Time: 50 Minutes

Ingredients:

- FOR THE TURKEY BREAST
- 2 teaspoons unsalted butter, at room temperature
- 1 bone-in split turkey breast (3 pounds), thawed if frozen
- 1 teaspoon poultry seasoning
- ½ teaspoon kosher salt
- ⅓ teaspoon freshly ground black pepper
- FOR THE GREEN BEAN CASSEROLE
- 1 (10.5-ounce) can condensed cream of mushroom soup
- ½ cup whole milk
- 1 cup store-bought crispy fried onions, divided
- ¼ teaspoon kosher salt
- ¼ teaspoon freshly ground black pepper
- 1 pound green beans, trimmed
- ¼ cup panko bread crumbs
- Nonstick cooking spray

Directions:

1. To prep the turkey breast: Spread the butter over the skin side of the turkey. Season with the poultry seasoning, salt, and black pepper.
2. To prep the green bean casserole: In a medium bowl, combine the soup, milk, ½ cup of crispy onions, the salt, and black pepper.
3. To cook the turkey and beans: Install a crisper plate in the Zone 1 basket. Place the turkey skin-side up in the basket and insert the basket in the unit. Place the green beans in the Zone 2 basket and insert the basket in the unit.
4. Select Zone 1, select AIR FRY, set the temperature to 360°F, and set the time to 50 minutes.
5. Select Zone 2, select ROAST, set the temperature to 350°F, and set the time to 40 minutes. Select SMART FINISH.
6. Press START/PAUSE to begin cooking.
7. When the Zone 2 timer reads 30 minutes, press START/PAUSE. Remove the basket and stir the soup mixture into the beans. Scatter the panko and remaining ½ cup of crispy onions over the top, then spritz with cooking spray. Reinsert the basket and press START/PAUSE to resume cooking.
8. When cooking is complete, the turkey will be cooked through (an instant-read thermometer should read 165°F) and the green bean casserole will be bubbling and golden brown on top.
9. Let the turkey and casserole rest for at least 15 minutes before serving.

Nutrition Info:

- (Per serving) Calories: 577; Total fat: 22g; Saturated fat: 6.5g; Carbohydrates: 24g; Fiber: 3.5g; Protein: 68g; Sodium: 1,165mg

Chili Chicken Wings

Servings: 4 | Cooking Time: 43 Minutes.

Ingredients:

- 8 chicken wings drumettes
- cooking spray
- ⅛ cup low-fat buttermilk
- ¼ cup almond flour
- McCormick Chicken Seasoning to taste
- Thai Chili Marinade
- 1 ½ tablespoons low-sodium soy sauce
- ½ teaspoon ginger, minced
- 1 ½ garlic cloves
- 1 green onion
- ½ teaspoon rice wine vinegar
- ½ tablespoon Sriracha sauce
- ½ tablespoon sesame oil

Directions:

1. Put all the ingredients for the marinade in the blender and blend them for 1 minute.
2. Keep this marinade aside. Pat dry the washed chicken and place it in the Ziploc bag.
3. Add buttermilk, chicken seasoning, and zip the bag.
4. Shake the bag well, then refrigerator for 30 minutes for marination.
5. Remove the chicken drumettes from the marinade, then dredge them through dry flour.
6. Spread the drumettes in the two crisper plate and spray them with cooking oil.
7. Return the crisper plate to the Ninja Foodi Dual Zone Air Fryer.
8. Choose the Air Fry mode for Zone 1 and set the temperature to 390 degrees F and the time to 43 minutes.
9. Select the "MATCH" button to copy the settings for Zone 2.
10. Initiate cooking by pressing the START/STOP button.
11. Toss the drumettes once cooked halfway through.
12. Now brush the chicken pieces with Thai chili sauce and then resume cooking.
13. Serve warm.

Nutrition Info:

- (Per serving) Calories 223 | Fat 11.7g |Sodium 721mg | Carbs 13.6g | Fiber 0.7g | Sugar 8g | Protein 15.7g

Chicken Fajitas With Street Corn

Servings:4 | Cooking Time: 20 Minutes

Ingredients:

- FOR THE FAJITAS
- 1½ pounds boneless, skinless chicken breasts, cut into strips
- 2 bell peppers (red, orange, yellow, or a combination), sliced into ½-inch-wide strips
- 1 small red onion, sliced
- 1 tablespoon vegetable oil
- 2 teaspoons chili powder
- 1 teaspoon ground cumin
- 1 teaspoon kosher salt
- ½ teaspoon freshly ground black pepper
- ½ teaspoon paprika
- ¼ cup fresh cilantro, chopped
- Juice of 1 lime
- 8 (6-inch) flour tortillas
- FOR THE CORN
- ¼ cup mayonnaise
- ¼ cup sour cream
- ¼ cup crumbled Cotija or feta cheese
- 2 tablespoons chopped fresh cilantro
- 1 teaspoon minced garlic
- ½ teaspoon chili powder
- 4 ears corn, husked

Directions:

1. To prep the fajitas: In a large bowl, combine the chicken, bell peppers, onion, oil, chili powder, cumin, salt, black pepper, and paprika and toss to coat.
2. To prep the corn: In a shallow dish, combine the mayonnaise, sour cream, cheese, cilantro, garlic, and chili powder. Mix well and set aside.
3. To cook the fajitas and corn: Install a crisper plate in each of the two baskets. Place the fajita filling in the Zone 1 basket and insert the basket in the unit. Place the corn ears in the Zone 2 basket and insert the basket in the unit.
4. Select Zone 1, select AIR FRY, set the temperature to 390°F, and set the time to 20 minutes.
5. Select Zone 2, select AIR BROIL, set the temperature to 450°F, and set the time to 12 minutes. Select SMART FINISH.
6. Press START/PAUSE to begin cooking.
7. When both timers read 6 minutes, press START/PAUSE. Remove the Zone 1 basket, shake to redistribute the fajita filling, and reinsert the basket. Remove the Zone 2 basket and use silicone-tipped tongs to flip the corn. Reinsert the basket and press START/PAUSE to resume cooking.
8. When cooking is complete, the chicken will be fully cooked and the vegetables will be slightly charred.
9. Mix the cilantro and lime juice into the fajita filling. Divide the filling among the tortillas. Roll the corn in the mayonnaise and cheese mixture to coat. Serve hot.

Nutrition Info:

- (Per serving) Calories: 705; Total fat: 29g; Saturated fat: 8g; Carbohydrates: 60g; Fiber: 5g; Protein: 51g; Sodium: 1,155mg

Thai Curry Chicken Kabobs

Servings: 4 | Cooking Time: 15 Minutes

Ingredients:

- 900g skinless chicken thighs
- 120ml Tamari
- 60ml coconut milk
- 3 tablespoons lime juice
- 3 tablespoons maple syrup
- 2 tablespoons Thai red curry

Directions:

1. Mix red curry paste, honey, lime juice, coconut milk, soy sauce in a bowl.
2. Add this sauce and chicken to a Ziplock bag.
3. Seal the bag and shake it to coat well.
4. Refrigerate the chicken for 2 hours then thread the chicken over wooden skewers.
5. Divide the skewers in the air fryer baskets.
6. Return the air fryer basket 1 to Zone 1, and basket 2 to Zone 2 of the Ninja Foodi 2-Basket Air Fryer.
7. Choose the "Air Fry" mode for Zone 1 at 350 degrees F and 15 minutes of cooking time.
8. Select the "MATCH COOK" option to copy the settings for Zone 2.
9. Initiate cooking by pressing the START/PAUSE BUTTON.
10. Flip the skewers once cooked halfway through.
11. Serve warm.

Nutrition Info:

- (Per serving) Calories 353 | Fat 5g |Sodium 818mg | Carbs 53.2g | Fiber 4.4g | Sugar 8g | Protein 17.3g

Beef, Pork, And
Lamb Recipes

Steak And Mashed Creamy Potatoes

Servings:1 | Cooking Time:45

Ingredients:

- 2 Russet potatoes, peeled and cubed
- ¼ cup butter, divided
- 1/3 cup heavy cream
- ½ cup shredded cheddar cheese
- Salt and black pepper, to taste
- 1 New York strip steak, about a pound
- 1 teaspoon of olive oil
- Oil spray, for greasing

Directions:

1. Rub the potatoes with salt and a little amount of olive oil about a teaspoon.
2. Next, season the steak with salt and black pepper.
3. Place the russet potatoes in a zone 1 basket.
4. Oil spray the steak from both sides and then place it in the zone 2 basket.
5. Set zone 1 to AIR fry mode for 45 minutes at 390 degrees F.
6. Set the zone 2 basket, at 12 minutes at 375 degrees F.
7. Hot start and Lethe ninja foodie do its magic.
8. One the cooking cycle completes, take out the steak and potatoes.
9. Mash the potatoes and then add butter, heavy cream, and cheese along with salt and black pepper.
10. Serve the mashed potatoes with steak.
11. Enjoy.

Nutrition Info:

- (Per serving) Calories1932 | Fat 85.2g| Sodium 3069mg | Carbs 82g | Fiber10.3 g| Sugar 5.3g | Protein 22.5g

Beef Kofta Kebab

Servings: 4 | Cooking Time: 18 Minutes

Ingredients:

- 455g ground beef
- ¼ cup white onion, grated
- ¼ cup parsley, chopped
- 1 tablespoon mint, chopped
- 2 cloves garlic, minced
- 1 teaspoon salt
- ½ teaspoon cumin
- 1 teaspoon oregano
- ½ teaspoon garlic salt
- 1 egg

Directions:

1. Mix ground beef with onion, parsley, mint, garlic, cumin, oregano, garlic salt and egg in a bowl.
2. Take 3 tbsp-sized beef kebabs out of this mixture.
3. Place the kebabs in the air fryer baskets.
4. Return the air fryer basket 1 to Zone 1, and basket 2 to Zone 2 of the Ninja Foodi 2-Basket Air Fryer.
5. Choose the "Air Fry" mode for Zone 1 at 375 degrees F and 18 minutes of cooking time.
6. Select the "MATCH COOK" option to copy the settings for Zone 2.
7. Initiate cooking by pressing the START/PAUSE BUTTON.
8. Flip the kebabs once cooked halfway through.
9. Serve warm.

Nutrition Info:

- (Per serving) Calories 316 | Fat 12.2g |Sodium 587mg | Carbs 12.2g | Fiber 1g | Sugar 1.8g | Protein 25.8g

Cheesesteak Taquitos

Servings: 8 | Cooking Time: 12 Minutes

Ingredients:

- 1 pack soft corn tortillas
- 136g beef steak strips
- 2 green peppers, sliced
- 1 white onion, chopped
- 1 pkg dry Italian dressing mix
- 10 slices Provolone cheese
- Cooking spray or olive oil

Directions:

1. Mix beef with cooking oil, peppers, onion, and dressing mix in a bowl.
2. Divide the strips in the air fryer baskets.
3. Return the air fryer basket 1 to Zone 1, and basket 2 to Zone 2 of the Ninja Foodi 2-Basket Air Fryer.
4. Choose the "Air Fry" mode for Zone 1 at 375 degrees F and 12 minutes of cooking time.
5. Select the "MATCH COOK" option to copy the settings for Zone 2.
6. Initiate cooking by pressing the START/PAUSE BUTTON.
7. Flip the strips once cooked halfway through.
8. Divide the beef strips in the tortillas and top the beef with a beef slice.

9. Roll the tortillas and serve.

Nutrition Info:

- (Per serving) Calories 410 | Fat 17.8g |Sodium 619mg | Carbs 21g | Fiber 1.4g | Sugar 1.8g | Protein 38.4g

Barbecue Ribs With Roasted Green Beans And Shallots

Servings:4 | Cooking Time: 40 Minutes

Ingredients:

- FOR THE RIBS
- 1 tablespoon light brown sugar
- 1 tablespoon smoked paprika
- 1 tablespoon chili powder
- 2 teaspoons kosher salt
- 1 teaspoon freshly ground black pepper
- 1 teaspoon garlic powder
- ¼ teaspoon cayenne pepper (optional)
- 2 pounds pork ribs
- 1 cup barbecue sauce (your favorite), for serving
- FOR THE GREEN BEANS AND SHALLOTS
- 1 pound green beans, trimmed
- 2 shallots, sliced
- 1 tablespoon olive oil
- ¼ teaspoon kosher salt

Directions:

1. To prep the ribs: In a small bowl, combine the brown sugar, paprika, chili powder, salt, black pepper, garlic powder, and cayenne (if using).
2. Rub the spice blend all over both sides of the ribs.
3. To prep the green beans and shallots: In a large bowl, combine the green beans, shallots, and oil. Toss to coat. Season with the salt.
4. To cook the ribs and vegetables: Install a crisper plate in each of the two baskets. Place the ribs in the Zone 1 basket and insert the basket in the unit. Place the green beans in the Zone 2 basket and insert the basket in the unit.
5. Select Zone 1, select AIR FRY, set the temperature to 375°F, and set the time to 40 minutes.
6. Select Zone 2, select ROAST, set the temperature to 400°F, and set the time to 20 minutes. Select SMART FINISH.
7. Press START/PAUSE to begin cooking.
8. When the Zone 1 timer reads 10 minutes, press START/PAUSE. Increase the temperature of Zone 1 to 400°F. Press START/PAUSE to resume cooking.
9. When cooking is complete, an instant-read thermometer inserted into the ribs should read 170°F and the green beans should be tender-crisp. Serve topped with your favorite barbecue sauce.

Nutrition Info:

- (Per serving) Calories: 541; Total fat: 27g; Saturated fat: 9g; Carbohydrates: 48g; Fiber: 4.5g; Protein: 28g; Sodium: 1,291mg

Steak In Air Fry

Servings:1 | Cooking Time:20

Ingredients:

- 2 teaspoons of canola oil
- 1 tablespoon of Montreal steaks seasoning
- 1 pound of beef steak

Directions:

1. The first step is to season the steak on both sides with canola oil and then rub a generous amount of steak seasoning all over.
2. We are using the AIR BROIL feature of the ninja air fryer and it works with one basket.
3. Put the steak in the basket and set it to AIR BROIL at 450 degrees F for 20 -22 minutes.
4. After 7 minutes, hit pause and take out the basket to flip the steak, and cover it with foil on top, for the remaining 14 minutes.
5. Once done, serve the medium-rare steak and enjoy it by resting for 10 minutes.
6. Serve by cutting in slices.
7. Enjoy.

Nutrition Info:

- (Per serving) Calories 935| Fat 37.2g| Sodium 1419mg | Carbs 0g | Fiber 0g| Sugar 0g | Protein137.5 g

Chinese Bbq Pork

Servings:35 | Cooking Time:25

Ingredients:

- 4 tablespoons of soy sauce
- ¼ cup red wine
- 2 tablespoons of oyster sauce
- ¼ tablespoons of hoisin sauce
- ¼ cup honey
- ¼ cup brown sugar
- Pinch of salt
- Pinch of black pepper
- 1 teaspoon of ginger garlic, paste
- 1 teaspoon of five-spice powder
- 1.5 pounds of pork shoulder, sliced

Directions:

1. Take a bowl and mix all the ingredients listed under sauce ingredients.
2. Transfer half of it to a sauce pan and let it cook for 10 minutes.
3. Set it aside.
4. Let the pork marinate in the remaining sauce for 2 hours.

5. Afterward, put the pork slices in the basket and set it to AIRBORIL mode 450 degrees for 25 minutes.
6. Make sure the internal temperature is above 160 degrees F once cooked.
7. If not add a few more minutes to the overall cooking time.
8. Once done, take it out and baste it with prepared sauce.
9. Serve and Enjoy.

Nutrition Info:

- (Per serving) Calories 1239| Fat 73 g| Sodium 2185 mg | Carbs 57.3 g | Fiber 0.4g| Sugar53.7 g | Protein 81.5 g

Balsamic Steak Tips With Roasted Asparagus And Mushroom Medley

Servings:4 | Cooking Time: 25 Minutes

Ingredients:

- FOR THE STEAK TIPS
- 1½ pounds sirloin tips
- ½ cup olive oil
- ¼ cup balsamic vinegar
- ¼ cup packed light brown sugar
- 1 tablespoon reduced-sodium soy sauce
- 1 teaspoon finely chopped fresh rosemary
- 1 teaspoon minced garlic
- FOR THE ASPARAGUS AND MUSHROOMS
- 6 ounces sliced cremini mushrooms
- 1 small red onion, sliced
- 1 tablespoon olive oil
- 1 pound asparagus, tough ends trimmed
- ⅛ teaspoon kosher salt

Directions:

1. To prep the steak tips: In a large bowl, combine the sirloin tips, oil, vinegar, brown sugar, soy sauce, rosemary, and garlic. Mix well to coat the steak.
2. To prep the mushrooms: In a large bowl, combine the mushrooms, onion, and oil.
3. To cook the steak and vegetables: Install a crisper plate in each of the two baskets. Shake any excess marinade from the steak tips, place the steak in the Zone 1 basket, and insert the basket in the unit. Place the mushrooms and onions in the Zone 2 basket and insert the basket in the unit.
4. Select Zone 1, select AIR FRY, set the temperature to 400°F, and set the time to 12 minutes.
5. Select Zone 2, select ROAST, set the temperature to 400°F, and set the time to 25 minutes. Select SMART FINISH.
6. Press START/PAUSE to begin cooking.
7. When the Zone 2 timer reads 10 minutes, press START/PAUSE. Remove the basket, add the asparagus to the mushrooms and onion, and sprinkle with salt. Reinsert the basket and press START/PAUSE to resume cooking.
8. When cooking is complete, the beef should be cooked to your liking and the asparagus crisp-tender. Serve warm.

Nutrition Info:

- (Per serving) Calories: 524; Total fat: 33g; Saturated fat: 2.5g; Carbohydrates: 16g; Fiber: 3g; Protein: 41g; Sodium: 192mg

Korean Bbq Beef

Servings: 6 | Cooking Time: 30 Minutes

Ingredients:

- For the meat:
- 1 pound flank steak or thinly sliced steak
- ¼ cup corn starch
- Coconut oil spray
- For the sauce:
- ½ cup soy sauce or gluten-free soy sauce
- ½ cup brown sugar
- 2 tablespoons white wine vinegar
- 1 clove garlic, crushed
- 1 tablespoon hot chili sauce
- 1 teaspoon ground ginger
- ½ teaspoon sesame seeds
- 1 tablespoon corn starch
- 1 tablespoon water

Directions:

1. To begin, prepare the steak. Thinly slice it in that toss it in the corn starch to be coated thoroughly. Spray the tops with some coconut oil.
2. Spray the crisping plates and drawers with the coconut oil.
3. Place the crisping plates into the drawers. Place the steak strips into each drawer. Insert both drawers into the unit.
4. Select zone 1, Select AIR FRY, set the temperature to 375 degrees F/ 190 degrees C, and set time to 30 minutes. Select MATCH to match zone 2 settings with zone 1. Press the START/STOP button to begin cooking.
5. While the steak is cooking, add the sauce ingredients EXCEPT for the corn starch and water to a medium saucepan.
6. Warm it up to a low boil, then whisk in the corn starch and water.
7. Carefully remove the steak and pour the sauce over. Mix well.

Nutrition Info:

- (Per serving) Calories 500 | Fat 19.8g | Sodium 680mg | Carbs 50.1g | Fiber 4.1g | Sugar 0g | Protein 27.9g

Curry-crusted Lamb Chops With Baked Brown Sugar Acorn Squash

Servings:4 | Cooking Time: 20 Minutes

Ingredients:

- FOR THE LAMB CHOPS
- 4 lamb loin chops (4 ounces each)
- 1 tablespoon olive oil
- 2 teaspoons curry powder
- ¼ teaspoon kosher salt
- FOR THE ACORN SQUASH
- 2 small acorn squash
- 4 teaspoons dark brown sugar
- 2 teaspoons salted butter
- ⅛ teaspoon kosher salt

Directions:

1. To prep the lamb chops: Brush both sides of the lamb chops with the oil and season with the curry powder and salt.
2. To prep the acorn squash: Cut the squash in half through the stem end and remove the seeds. Place 1 teaspoon of brown sugar and ½ teaspoon of butter into the well of each squash half.
3. To cook the lamb and squash: Install a crisper plate in each of the two baskets. Place the lamb chops in the Zone 1 basket and insert the basket in the unit. Place the squash cut-side up in the Zone 2 basket and insert the basket in the unit.
4. Select Zone 1, select AIR FRY, set the temperature to 400°F, and set the timer to 15 minutes.
5. Select Zone 2, select BAKE, set the temperature to 400°F, and set the time to 20 minutes. Select SMART FINISH.
6. Press START/PAUSE to begin cooking.
7. When both timers read 5 minutes, press START/PAUSE. Remove the Zone 1 basket and use a pair of silicone-tipped tongs to flip the lamb chops. Reinsert the basket in the unit. Remove the Zone 2 basket and spoon the melted butter and sugar over the top edges of the squash. Reinsert the basket and press START/PAUSE to resume cooking.
8. When cooking is complete, the lamb should be cooked to your liking and the squash soft when pierced with a fork.
9. Remove the lamb chops from the basket and let rest for 5 minutes. Season the acorn squash with salt before serving.

Nutrition Info:

- (Per serving) Calories: 328; Total fat: 19g; Saturated fat: 7.5g; Carbohydrates: 23g; Fiber: 3g; Protein: 16g; Sodium: 172mg

Air Fried Lamb Chops

Servings: 4 | Cooking Time: 10 Minutes

Ingredients:

- 700g lamb chops
- ½ teaspoon oregano
- 3 tablespoons parsley, minced
- ½ teaspoon black pepper
- 3 cloves garlic minced
- 2 tablespoons lemon juice
- 2 tablespoons olive oil
- Salt to taste

Directions:

1. Pat dry the chops and mix with lemon juice and the rest of the ingredients.
2. Place these chops in the air fryer baskets.
3. Return the air fryer basket 1 to Zone 1, and basket 2 to Zone 2 of the Ninja Foodi 2-Basket Air Fryer.
4. Choose the "Air Fry" mode for Zone 1and set the temperature to 400 degrees F and 10 minutes of cooking time.
5. Select the "MATCH COOK" option to copy the settings for Zone 2.
6. Initiate cooking by pressing the START/PAUSE BUTTON.
7. Flip the pork chops once cooked halfway through.
8. Serve warm.

Nutrition Info:

- (Per serving) Calories 396 | Fat 23.2g |Sodium 622mg | Carbs 0.7g | Fiber 0g | Sugar 0g | Protein 45.6g

Pork Chops

Servings:2 | Cooking Time:17

Ingredients:

- 1 tablespoon of rosemary, chopped
- Salt and black pepper, to taste
- 2 garlic cloves
- 1-inch ginger
- 2 tablespoons of olive oil
- 8 pork chops

Directions:

1. Take a blender and pulse together rosemary, salt, pepper, garlic cloves, ginger, and olive oil.
2. Rub this marinade over pork chops and let it rest for 1 hour.
3. Then divide it amongst air fryer baskets and set it to AIR FRY mode for 17 minutes at 375 degrees F.
4. Once the cooking cycle is done, take out and serve hot.

Nutrition Info:

- (Per serving) Calories 1154| Fat 93.8g| Sodium 225mg | Carbs 2.1g | Fiber0.8 g| Sugar 0g | Protein 72.2g

Tomahawk Steak

Servings: 4 | Cooking Time: 12 Minutes

Ingredients:

- 4 tablespoons butter, softened
- 2 cloves garlic, minced
- 2 teaspoons chopped fresh parsley
- 1 teaspoon chopped chives
- 1 teaspoon chopped fresh thyme
- 1 teaspoon chopped fresh rosemary
- 2 (2 pounds each) bone-in ribeye steaks
- Kosher salt, to taste
- Freshly ground black pepper, to taste

Directions:

1. In a small bowl, combine the butter and herbs. Place the mixture in the center of a piece of plastic wrap and roll it into a log. Twist the ends together to keep it tight and refrigerate until hardened, about 20 minutes.
2. Season the steaks on both sides with salt and pepper.
3. Install a crisper plate in both drawers. Place one steak in the zone 1 drawer and one in zone 2's, then insert the drawers into the unit.
4. Select zone 1, select AIR FRY, set temperature to 390 degrees F/ 200 degrees C, and set time to 12 minutes. Select MATCH to match zone 2 settings to zone 1. Press the START/STOP button to begin cooking.
5. When the time reaches 10 minutes, press START/STOP to pause the unit. Remove the drawers and flip the steaks. Add the herb-butter to the tops of the steaks. Re-insert the drawers into the unit and press START/STOP to resume cooking.
6. Serve and enjoy!

Nutrition Info:

- (Per serving) Calories 338 | Fat 21.2g | Sodium 1503mg | Carbs 5.1g | Fiber 0.3g | Sugar 4.6g | Protein 29.3g

Beef Ribs Ii

Servings:2 | Cooking Time:1

Ingredients:

- ¼ cup olive oil
- 4 garlic cloves, minced
- ½ cup white wine vinegar
- ¼ cup soy sauce, reduced-sodium
- ¼ cup Worcestershire sauce
- 1 lemon juice
- Salt and black pepper, to taste
- 2 tablespoons of Italian seasoning
- 1 teaspoon of smoked paprika
- 2 tablespoons of mustard
- ½ cup maple syrup
- Meat Ingredients:
- Oil spray, for greasing
- 8 beef ribs lean

Directions:

1. Take a large bowl and add all the ingredients under marinade ingredients.
2. Put the marinade in a zip lock bag and add ribs to it.
3. Let it sit for 4 hours.
4. Now take out the basket of air fryer and grease the baskets with oil spray.
5. Now dived the ribs among two baskets.
6. Set it to AIR fry mode at 220 degrees F for 30 minutes.
7. Select Pause and take out the baskets.
8. Afterward, flip the ribs and cook for 30 minutes at 250 degrees F.
9. Once done, serve the juicy and tender ribs.
10. Enjoy.

Nutrition Info:

- (Per serving) Calories 1927| Fat116g| Sodium 1394mg | Carbs 35.2g | Fiber 1.3g| Sugar29 g | Protein 172.3g

Tasty Lamb Patties

Servings: 8 | Cooking Time: 12 Minutes

Ingredients:

- 900g ground lamb
- 1 tbsp ground coriander
- 4g fresh parsley, chopped
- 1 tsp garlic, minced
- ½ tsp cinnamon
- 1 tsp paprika
- 1 tbsp ground cumin
- Pepper
- Salt

Directions:

1. Add ground meat and remaining ingredients into a bowl and mix until well combined.
2. Insert a crisper plate in the Ninja Foodi air fryer baskets.
3. Make patties from the meat mixture and place in both baskets.
4. Select zone 1, then select "air fry" mode and set the temperature to 390 degrees F for 12 minutes. Press "match" to match zone 2 settings to zone 1. Press "start/stop" to begin. Turn halfway through.

Nutrition Info:

- (Per serving) Calories 216 | Fat 8.5g |Sodium 108mg | Carbs 0.8g | Fiber 0.3g | Sugar 0.1g | Protein 32.1g

Bacon Wrapped Pork Tenderloin

Servings: 2 | Cooking Time: 20 Minutes

Ingredients:

- ½ teaspoon salt
- ¼ teaspoon black pepper
- 1 pork tenderloin
- 6 center cut strips bacon
- cooking string

Directions:

1. Cut two bacon strips in half and place them on the working surface.
2. Place the other bacon strips on top and lay the tenderloin over the bacon strip.
3. Wrap the bacon around the tenderloin and tie the roast with a kitchen string.
4. Place the roast in the first air fryer basket.
5. Return the air fryer basket 1 to Zone 1, and basket 2 to Zone 2 of the Ninja Foodi 2-Basket Air Fryer.
6. Choose the "Air Fry" mode for Zone 1 and set the temperature to 400 degrees F and 20 minutes of cooking time.
7. Initiate cooking by pressing the START/PAUSE BUTTON.
8. Slice and serve warm.

Nutrition Info:

- (Per serving) Calories 459 | Fat 17.7g |Sodium 1516mg | Carbs 1.7g | Fiber 0.5g | Sugar 0.4g | Protein 69.2g

Garlic Butter Steaks

Servings: 2 | Cooking Time: 25 Minutes

Ingredients:

- 2 (6 ounces each) sirloin steaks or ribeyes
- 2 tablespoons unsalted butter
- 1 clove garlic, crushed
- ½ teaspoon dried parsley
- ½ teaspoon dried rosemary
- Salt and pepper, to taste

Directions:

1. Season the steaks with salt and pepper and set them to rest for about 2 hours before cooking.
2. Put the butter in a bowl. Add the garlic, parsley, and rosemary. Allow the butter to soften.
3. Whip together with a fork or spoon once the butter has softened.
4. When you're ready to cook, install a crisper plate in both drawers. Place the sirloin steaks in a single layer in each drawer. Insert the drawers into the unit.
5. Select zone 1, select AIR FRY, set temperature to 360 degrees F/ 180 degrees C, and set time to 10 minutes. Select MATCH to match zone 2 settings to zone 1. Select START/STOP to begin.
6. Once done, serve with the garlic butter.

Nutrition Info:

- (Per serving) Calories 519 | Fat 36g | Sodium 245mg | Carbs 1g | Fiber 0g | Sugar 0g | Protein 46g

Bell Peppers With Sausages

Servings:4 | Cooking Time:20

Ingredients:

- 6 beef or pork Italian sausages
- 4 bell peppers, whole
- Oil spray, for greasing
- 2 cups of cooked rice
- 1 cup of sour cream

Directions:

1. Put the bell pepper in the zone 1 basket and sausages in the zone 2 basket of the air fryer.
2. Set zone 1 to AIR FRY MODE for 10 minutes at 400 degrees F.
3. For zone 2 set it to 20 minutes at 375 degrees F.
4. Hit the smart finish button, so both finish at the same time.
5. After 5 minutes take out the sausage basket and break or mince it with a plastic spatula.
6. Then, let the cooking cycle finish.
7. Once done serve the minced meat with bell peppers and serve over cooked rice with a dollop of sour cream.

Nutrition Info:

- (Per serving) Calories1356 | Fat 81.2g| Sodium 3044 mg | Carbs 96g | Fiber 3.1g | Sugar 8.3g | Protein 57.2 g

Spicy Lamb Chops

Servings:4 | Cooking Time:15

Ingredients:

- 12 lamb chops, bone-in
- Salt and black pepper, to taste
- ½ teaspoon of lemon zest
- 1 tablespoon of lemon juice
- 1 teaspoon of paprika
- 1 teaspoon of garlic powder
- ½ teaspoon of Italian seasoning
- ¼ teaspoon of onion powder

Directions:

1. Add the lamb chops to the bowl and sprinkle salt, garlic powder, Italian seasoning, onion powder, black pepper, lemon zest, lemon juice, and paprika.
2. Rub the chops well, and divide it between both the baskets of the air fryer.
3. Set zone 1 basket to 400 degrees F, for 15 minutes at AIR FRY mode.
4. Select MATCH for zone2 basket.
5. After 10 minutes, take out the baskets and flip the

chops cook for the remaining minutes, and then serve.

Nutrition Info:

- (Per serving) Calories 787| Fat 45.3g| Sodium1 mg | Carbs 16.1g | Fiber0.3g | Sugar 0.4g | Protein 75.3g

Lamb Shank With Mushroom Sauce

Servings: 4 | Cooking Time: 35 Minutes.

Ingredients:

- 20 mushrooms, chopped
- 2 red bell pepper, chopped
- 2 red onion, chopped
- 1 cup red wine
- 4 leeks, chopped
- 6 tablespoons balsamic vinegar
- 2 teaspoons black pepper
- 2 teaspoons salt
- 3 tablespoons fresh rosemary
- 6 garlic cloves
- 4 lamb shanks
- 3 tablespoons olive oil

Directions:

1. Season the lamb shanks with salt, pepper, rosemary, and 1 teaspoon of olive oil.
2. Set half of the shanks in each of the crisper plate.
3. Return the crisper plate to the Ninja Foodi Dual Zone Air Fryer.
4. Choose the Air Fry mode for Zone 1 and set the temperature to 390 degrees F and the time to 25 minutes.
5. Select the "MATCH" button to copy the settings for Zone 2.
6. Initiate cooking by pressing the START/STOP button.
7. Flip the shanks halfway through, and resume cooking.
8. Meanwhile, add and heat the remaining olive oil in a skillet.
9. Add onion and garlic to sauté for 5 minutes.
10. Add in mushrooms and cook for 5 minutes.
11. Add red wine and cook until it is absorbed
12. Stir all the remaining vegetables along with black pepper and salt.
13. Cook until vegetables are al dente.
14. Serve the air fried shanks with sautéed vegetable fry.

Nutrition Info:

- (Per serving) Calories 352 | Fat 9.1g |Sodium 1294mg | Carbs 3.9g | Fiber 1g | Sugar 1g | Protein 61g

Steak Bites With Cowboy Butter

Servings: 4 | Cooking Time: 15 Minutes

Ingredients:

- 455g steak sirloin
- Cooking spray
- Cowboy butter sauce
- 1 stick salted butter melted
- 1 tablespoon lemon zest
- 1 tablespoon lemon juice
- ½ teaspoon garlic powder
- ¼ teaspoon red pepper flakes
- ½ teaspoon sea salt
- ½ teaspoon black pepper
- ½ tablespoon Dijon mustard
- ½ teaspoon Worcestershire sauce
- 1 tablespoon parsley freshly chopped

Directions:

1. Mix all the cowboy butter ingredients in a bowl.
2. Stir in steak cubes and mix well.
3. Cover and marinate in the refrigerator for 1 hour.
4. Divide the steak cubes in the air fryer baskets then use cooking spray.
5. Return the air fryer basket 1 to Zone 1, and basket 2 to Zone 2 of the Ninja Foodi 2-Basket Air Fryer.
6. Choose the "Air Fry" mode for Zone 1 at 400 degrees F and 15 minutes of cooking time.
7. Select the "MATCH COOK" option to copy the settings for Zone 2.
8. Initiate cooking by pressing the START/PAUSE BUTTON.
9. Serve warm.

Nutrition Info:

- (Per serving) Calories 264 | Fat 17g |Sodium 129mg | Carbs 0.9g | Fiber 0.3g | Sugar 0g | Protein 27g

Zucchini Pork Skewers

Servings: 4 | Cooking Time: 23 Minutes.

Ingredients:

- 1 large zucchini, cut 1" pieces
- 1 lb. boneless pork belly, cut into cubes
- 1 onion yellow, diced in squares
- 1 ½ cups grape tomatoes
- 1 garlic clove minced
- 1 lemon, juice only
- ¼ cup olive oil
- 2 tablespoons balsamic vinegar
- 1 teaspoon oregano
- olive oil spray

Directions:

1. Mix together balsamic vinegar, garlic, oregano lemon juice, and ¼ cup of olive oil in a suitable bowl.
2. Then toss in diced pork pieces and mix well to coat.
3. Leave the seasoned pork to marinate for 60 minutes in the refrigerator.
4. Take suitable wooden skewers for your Ninja Foodi Dual Zone Air Fryer's drawer, and then thread marinated pork and vegetables on each skewer in an alternating manner.
5. Place half of the skewers in each of the crisper plate and spray them with cooking oil.
6. Return the crisper plate to the Ninja Foodi Dual Zone Air Fryer.
7. Choose the Air Fry mode for Zone 1 and set the temperature to 390 degrees F and the time to 23 minutes.
8. Select the "MATCH" button to copy the settings for Zone 2.
9. Initiate cooking by pressing the START/STOP button.
10. Flip the skewers once cooked halfway through, and resume cooking.
11. Serve warm.

Nutrition Info:

- (Per serving) Calories 459 | Fat 17.7g |Sodium 1516mg | Carbs 1.7g | Fiber 0.5g | Sugar 0.4g | Protein 69.2g

Sausage Meatballs

Servings: 24 | Cooking Time: 10 Minutes

Ingredients:

- 1 egg, lightly beaten
- 900g pork sausage
- 29g breadcrumbs
- 100g pimientos, drained & diced
- 1 tsp curry powder
- 1 tbsp garlic, minced
- 30ml olive oil
- 1 tbsp fresh rosemary, minced
- 25g parsley, minced
- Pepper
- Salt

Directions:

1. In a bowl, add pork sausage and remaining ingredients and mix until well combined.
2. Insert a crisper plate in the Ninja Foodi air fryer baskets.
3. Make small balls from the meat mixture and place them in both baskets.
4. Select zone 1 then select "air fry" mode and set the temperature to 390 degrees F for 10 minutes. Press "match" to match zone 2 settings to zone 1. Press "start/stop" to begin.

Nutrition Info:

- (Per serving) Calories 153 | Fat 12.2g |Sodium 303mg | Carbs 2.6g | Fiber 0.4g | Sugar 1.1g | Protein 8g

Easy Breaded Pork Chops

Servings: 8 | Cooking Time: 12 Minutes

Ingredients:

- 1 egg
- 118ml milk
- 8 pork chops
- 1 packet ranch seasoning
- 238g breadcrumbs
- Pepper
- Salt

Directions:

1. In a small bowl, whisk the egg and milk.
2. In a separate shallow dish, mix breadcrumbs, ranch seasoning, pepper, and salt.
3. Dip each pork chop in the egg mixture, then coat with breadcrumbs.
4. Insert a crisper plate in the Ninja Foodi air fryer baskets.
5. Place the coated pork chops in both baskets.
6. Select zone 1, then select air fry mode and set the temperature to 360 degrees F for 12 minutes. Press "match" to match zone 2 settings to zone 1. Press "start/stop" to

begin. Turn halfway through.

Nutrition Info:

- (Per serving) Calories 378 | Fat 22.2g |Sodium 298mg | Carbs 20.2g | Fiber 1.2g | Sugar 2.4g | Protein 22.8g

Short Ribs & Root Vegetables

Servings:2 | Cooking Time:45

Ingredients:

- 1 pound of beef short ribs, bone-in and trimmed
- Salt and black pepper, to taste
- 2 tablespoons canola oil, divided
- 1/4 cup red wine
- 3 tablespoons brown sugar
- 2 cloves garlic, peeled, minced
- 4 carrots, peeled, cut into 1-inch pieces
- 2 parsnips, peeled, cut into 1-inch pieces
- ½ cup pearl onions

Directions:

1. Season the ribs with salt and black pepper and rub a little amount of canola oil on both sides.
2. Place it in zone 1 basket of the air fryer.
3. Next, take a bowl and add pearl onions, parsnip, carrots, garlic, brown sugar, red wine, salt, and black pepper.
4. Add the vegetable mixture to the zone 2 basket.
5. Set the zone 1 basket time to 12 minutes at 375 degrees F at AIR FRY mode.
6. Set the zone 2 basket at AIR FRY mode at 390 degrees F for 18 minutes.
7. Hit start so the cooking cycle being.
8. Once the cooking complete, take out the ingredient and serve short ribs with the mixed vegetables and liquid collect at the bottom of zone 2 basket
9. Enjoy it hot.

Nutrition Info:

- (Per serving) Calories1262 | Fat 98.6g| Sodium 595mg | Carbs 57g | Fiber 10.1g| Sugar 28.2g | Protein 35.8g

Parmesan Pork Chops

Servings: 4 | Cooking Time: 15 Minutes.

Ingredients:

- 4 boneless pork chops
- 2 tablespoons olive oil
- ½ cup freshly grated Parmesan
- 1 teaspoon salt
- 1 teaspoon paprika
- 1 teaspoon garlic powder
- 1 teaspoon onion powder
- ½ teaspoon black pepper

Directions:

1. Pat dry the pork chops with a paper towel and rub them with olive oil.
2. Mix parmesan with spices in a medium bowl.
3. Rub the pork chops with Parmesan mixture.
4. Place 2 seasoned pork chops in each of the two crisper plate
5. Return the crisper plate to the Ninja Foodi Dual Zone Air Fryer.
6. Choose the Air Fry mode for Zone 1 and set the temperature to 390 degrees F and the time to 15 minutes.
7. Select the "MATCH" button to copy the settings for Zone 2.
8. Initiate cooking by pressing the START/STOP button.
9. Flip the pork chops when cooked halfway through, then resume cooking.
10. Serve warm.

Nutrition Info:

- (Per serving) Calories 396 | Fat 23.2g |Sodium 622mg | Carbs 0.7g | Fiber 0g | Sugar 0g | Protein 45.6g

Marinated Pork Chops

Servings: 2 | Cooking Time: 12 Minutes

Ingredients:

- 2 pork chops, boneless
- 18g sugar
- 1 tbsp water
- 15ml rice wine
- 15ml dark soy sauce
- 15ml light soy sauce
- ½ tsp cinnamon
- ½ tsp five-spice powder
- 1 tsp black pepper

Directions:

1. Add pork chops and remaining ingredients into a zip-lock bag. Seal the bag and place in the refrigerator for 4 hours.
2. Insert a crisper plate in the Ninja Foodi air fryer baskets.
3. Place the marinated pork chops in both baskets.
4. Select zone 1, then select air fry mode and set the temperature to 380 degrees F for 12 minutes. Press "match" to match zone 2 settings to zone 1. Press "start/stop" to begin.

Nutrition Info:

- (Per serving) Calories 306 | Fat 19.9g |Sodium 122mg | Carbs 13.7g | Fiber 0.6g | Sugar 11g | Protein 18.1g

Cilantro Lime Steak

Servings: 4 | Cooking Time: 10 Minutes

Ingredients:

- 450g flank steak, sliced
- 1 tsp cumin
- 1 tsp olive oil
- 4 tsp soy sauce
- 12g cilantro, chopped
- ¼ tsp cayenne
- 45ml lime juice
- 2 tsp chilli powder
- ¼ tsp salt

Directions:

1. Add the sliced steak pieces and the remaining ingredients into a zip-lock bag. Seal the bag and place in the refrigerator for 2 hours.
2. Insert a crisper plate in the Ninja Foodi air fryer baskets.
3. Place the marinated steak pieces in both baskets.
4. Select zone 1, then select "air fry" mode and set the temperature to 380 degrees F for 10 minutes. Press "match" to match zone 2 settings to zone 1. Press "start/stop" to begin.

Nutrition Info:

- (Per serving) Calories 240 | Fat 11g |Sodium 524mg | Carbs 1.5g | Fiber 0.6g | Sugar 0.2g | Protein 32.2g

Pork Tenderloin With Brown Sugar–pecan Sweet Potatoes

Servings:4 | Cooking Time: 45 Minutes

Ingredients:

- FOR THE PORK TENDERLOIN
- 1½ pounds pork tenderloin
- 2 teaspoons vegetable oil
- ½ teaspoon kosher salt
- ½ teaspoon poultry seasoning
- FOR THE SWEET POTATOES
- 4 teaspoons unsalted butter, at room temperature
- 2 tablespoons dark brown sugar
- ¼ cup chopped pecans
- 4 small sweet potatoes

Directions:

1. To prep the pork: Coat the pork tenderloin with the oil, then rub with the salt and poultry seasoning.
2. To prep the sweet potatoes: In a small bowl, mix the butter, brown sugar, and pecans until well combined.
3. To cook the pork and sweet potatoes: Install a crisper plate in the Zone 1 basket. Place the pork tenderloin in the basket and insert the basket in the unit. Place the sweet potatoes in the Zone 2 basket and insert the basket in the unit.
4. Select Zone 1, select AIR FRY, set the temperature to 390°F, and set the time to 25 minutes.
5. Select Zone 2, select BAKE, set the temperature to 400°F, and set the time to 45 minutes. Select SMART FINISH.
6. Press START/PAUSE to begin cooking.
7. When the Zone 2 timer reads 10 minutes, press START/PAUSE. Remove the basket. Slice the sweet potatoes open lengthwise. Divide the pecan mixture among the potatoes. Reinsert the basket and press START/PAUSE to resume cooking.
8. When cooking is complete, the pork will be cooked through (an instant-read thermometer should read 145°F) and the potatoes will be soft and their flesh fluffy.
9. Transfer the pork loin to a plate or cutting board and let rest for at least 5 minutes before slicing and serving.

Nutrition Info:

- (Per serving) Calories: 415; Total fat: 15g; Saturated fat: 4.5g; Carbohydrates: 33g; Fiber: 4.5g; Protein: 36g; Sodium: 284mg

Fish And Seafood Recipes

Crispy Catfish

Servings: 4 | Cooking Time: 17 Minutes.

Ingredients:

- 4 catfish fillets
- ¼ cup Louisiana Fish fry
- 1 tablespoon olive oil
- 1 tablespoon parsley, chopped
- 1 lemon, sliced
- Fresh herbs, to garnish

Directions:

1. Mix fish fry with olive oil, and parsley then liberally rub over the catfish.
2. Place two fillets in each of the crisper plate.
3. Return the crisper plates to the Ninja Foodi Dual Zone Air Fryer.
4. Choose the Air Fry mode for Zone 1 and set the temperature to 390 degrees F and the time to 17 minutes.
5. Select the "MATCH" button to copy the settings for Zone 2.
6. Initiate cooking by pressing the START/STOP button.
7. Garnish with lemon slices and herbs.
8. Serve warm.

Nutrition Info:

- (Per serving) Calories 275 | Fat 1.4g |Sodium 582mg | Carbs 31.5g | Fiber 1.1g | Sugar 0.1g | Protein 29.8g

Honey Teriyaki Tilapia

Servings: 4 | Cooking Time: 10 Minutes

Ingredients:

- 8 tablespoons low-sodium teriyaki sauce
- 3 tablespoons honey
- 2 garlic cloves, minced
- 2 tablespoons extra virgin olive oil
- 3 pieces tilapia (each cut into 2 pieces)

Directions:

1. Combine all the first 4 ingredients to make the marinade.
2. Pour the marinade over the tilapia and let it sit for 20 minutes.
3. Place a crisper plate in each drawer. Place the tilapia in the drawers. Insert the drawers into the unit.
4. Select zone 1, then AIR FRY, then set the temperature to 360 degrees F/ 180 degrees C with a 10-minute timer. To match zone 2 settings to zone 1, choose MATCH. To begin, select START/STOP.
5. Remove the tilapia from the drawers after the timer has finished.

Nutrition Info:

- (Per serving) Calories 350 | Fat 16.4g | Sodium 706mg | Carbs 19.3g | Fiber 0.1g | Sugar 19g | Protein 29.3g

Sesame Honey Salmon

Servings: 4 | Cooking Time: 10minutes

Ingredients:

- 4 salmon fillets
- 85g honey
- 15ml sesame oil
- 1 tbsp garlic, minced
- 2 tbsp soy sauce
- 1 tbsp sriracha
- Pepper
- Salt

Directions:

1. In a bowl, coat fish fillets with oil, garlic, honey, sriracha, soy sauce, pepper, and salt. Cover and place in refrigerator for 30 minutes.
2. Insert a crisper plate in the Ninja Foodi air fryer baskets.
3. Place the marinated fish fillets in both baskets.
4. Select zone 1, then select "air fry" mode and set the temperature to 375 degrees F for 10 minutes. Press "match" to match zone 2 settings to zone 1. Press "start/stop" to begin.

Nutrition Info:

- (Per serving) Calories 341 | Fat 14.4g |Sodium 596mg | Carbs 19.5g | Fiber 0.2g | Sugar 17.6g | Protein 35.2g

Healthy Lobster Cakes

Servings: 6 | Cooking Time: 12 Minutes

Ingredients:

- 1 egg
- 145g cooked lobster meat
- 60g butter, melted
- 1 tbsp Cajun seasoning
- 50g breadcrumbs
- Pepper
- Salt

Directions:

1. In a shallow dish, add breadcrumbs, pepper, and salt.
2. In a bowl, mix lobster meat, Cajun seasoning, egg, and butter until well combined.
3. Make patties from the lobster meat mixture and coat with breadcrumbs.
4. Insert a crisper plate in the Ninja Foodi air fryer baskets.
5. Place the coated patties in both baskets.
6. Select zone 1, then select "bake" mode and set the temperature to 390 degrees F for 12 minutes. Press "match" to match zone 2 settings to zone 1. Press "start/stop" to begin.

Nutrition Info:

- (Per serving) Calories 119 | Fat 7.2g |Sodium 287mg | Carbs 6.6g | Fiber 0.4g | Sugar 0.6g | Protein 6.8g

Tuna Steaks

Servings: 2 | Cooking Time: 30 Minutes

Ingredients:

- 2 (6 ounce) boneless tuna steaks
- ¼ cup soy sauce
- 2 teaspoons honey
- 1 teaspoon grated ginger
- 1 teaspoon sesame oil
- ½ teaspoon rice vinegar

Directions:

1. Mix rice vinegar, sesame oil, ginger, honey and soy sauce in a bowl.
2. Pour this marinade over the tuna steaks and cover to marinate for 30 minutes.
3. Place the tuna steaks in the air fryer baskets in a single layer.
4. Return the air fryer basket 1 to Zone 1, and basket 2 to Zone 2 of the Ninja Foodi 2-Basket Air Fryer.
5. Choose the "Air Fry" mode for Zone 1 and set the temperature to 380 degrees F and 4 minutes of cooking time.
6. Select the "MATCH COOK" option to copy the settings for Zone 2.
7. Initiate cooking by pressing the START/PAUSE BUTTON.
8. Serve warm.

Nutrition Info:

- (Per serving) Calories 348 | Fat 30g |Sodium 660mg | Carbs 5g | Fiber 0g | Sugar 0g | Protein 14g

Herb Tuna Patties

Servings: 10 | Cooking Time: 12 Minutes

Ingredients:

- 2 eggs
- 425g can tuna, drained & diced
- ½ tsp garlic powder
- ½ small onion, minced
- 1 celery stalk, chopped
- 42g parmesan cheese, grated
- 50g breadcrumbs
- ½ tsp dried oregano
- ½ tsp dried basil
- ½ tsp dried thyme
- 15ml lemon juice
- 1 lemon zest
- Pepper
- Salt

Directions:

1. In a bowl, mix tuna with remaining ingredients until well combined.
2. Insert a crisper plate in the Ninja Foodi air fryer baskets.
3. Make patties from the tuna mixture and place them in both baskets.
4. Select zone 1, then select "bake" mode and set the temperature to 380 degrees F for 12 minutes. Press "match" to match zone 2 settings to zone 1. Press "start/stop" to begin. Turn halfway through.

Nutrition Info:

- (Per serving) Calories 86 | Fat 1.5g |Sodium 90mg | Carbs 4.5g | Fiber 0.4g | Sugar 0.6g | Protein 12.8g

Shrimp Po'boys With Sweet Potato Fries

Servings:4 | Cooking Time: 30 Minutes

Ingredients:

- FOR THE SHRIMP PO'BOYS
- ½ cup buttermilk
- 1 tablespoon Louisiana-style hot sauce
- ¾ cup all-purpose flour
- ½ cup cornmeal
- ½ teaspoon kosher salt
- ½ teaspoon paprika
- ½ teaspoon garlic powder
- ½ teaspoon freshly ground black pepper
- 1 pound peeled medium shrimp, thawed if frozen
- Nonstock cooking spray
- ½ cup store-bought rémoulade sauce
- 4 French bread rolls, halved lengthwise
- ½ cup shredded lettuce
- 1 tomato, sliced
- FOR THE SWEET POTATO FRIES
- 2 medium sweet potatoes
- 2 teaspoons vegetable oil
- ¼ teaspoon garlic powder
- ¼ teaspoon paprika
- ¼ teaspoon kosher salt

Directions:

1. To prep the shrimp: In a medium bowl, combine the buttermilk and hot sauce. In a shallow bowl, combine the flour, cornmeal, salt, paprika, garlic powder, and black pepper.
2. Add the shrimp to the buttermilk and stir to coat. Remove the shrimp, letting the excess buttermilk drip off, then add to the cornmeal mixture to coat.
3. Spritz the breaded shrimp with cooking spray, then let sit for 10 minutes.
4. To prep the sweet potatoes: Peel the sweet potatoes and cut them lengthwise into ¼-inch-thick sticks (like shoestring fries).
5. In a large bowl, combine the sweet potatoes, oil, garlic powder, paprika, and salt. Toss to coat.
6. To cook the shrimp and fries: Install a crisper plate in each of the two baskets. Place the shrimp in the Zone 1 basket and insert the basket in the unit. Place the sweet potatoes in a single layer in the Zone 2 basket and insert the basket in the unit.
7. Select Zone 1, select AIR FRY, set the temperature to 390°F, and set the timer to 13 minutes.
8. Select Zone 2, select AIR FRY, set the temperature to 400°F, and set the timer to 30 minutes. Select SMART FINISH.
9. Press START/PAUSE to begin cooking.
10. When cooking is complete, the shrimp should be golden and cooked through and the sweet potato fries crisp.
11. Spread the rémoulade on the cut sides of the rolls. Divide the lettuce and tomato among the rolls, then top with the fried shrimp. Serve with the sweet potato fries on the side.

Nutrition Info:

- (Per serving) Calories: 669; Total fat: 22g; Saturated fat: 2g; Carbohydrates: 86g; Fiber: 3.5g; Protein: 33g; Sodium: 1,020mg

Herb Lemon Mussels

Servings: 6 | Cooking Time: 10 Minutes

Ingredients:

- 1kg mussels, steamed & half shell
- 1 tbsp thyme, chopped
- 1 tbsp parsley, chopped
- 1 tsp dried parsley
- 1 tsp garlic, minced
- 60ml olive oil
- 45ml lemon juice
- Pepper
- Salt

Directions:

1. In a bowl, mix mussels with the remaining ingredients.
2. Insert a crisper plate in the Ninja Foodi air fryer baskets.
3. Add the mussels to both baskets.
4. Select zone 1 then select "air fry" mode and set the temperature to 360 degrees F for 10 minutes. Press "match" to match zone 2 settings to zone 1. Press "start/stop" to begin.

Nutrition Info:

- (Per serving) Calories 206 | Fat 11.9g |Sodium 462mg | Carbs 6.3g | Fiber 0.3g | Sugar 0.2g | Protein 18.2g

Lemon Pepper Fish Fillets

Servings: 4 | Cooking Time: 10 Minutes

Ingredients:

- 4 tilapia fillets
- 30ml olive oil
- 2 tbsp lemon zest
- ⅛ tsp paprika
- 1 tsp garlic, minced
- 1 ½ tsp ground peppercorns
- Pepper
- Salt

Directions:

1. In a small bowl, mix oil, peppercorns, paprika, garlic, lemon zest, pepper, and salt.
2. Brush the fish fillets with oil mixture.
3. Insert a crisper plate in the Ninja Foodi air fryer baskets.
4. Place fish fillets in both baskets.
5. Select zone 1 then select "air fry" mode and set the temperature to 390 degrees F for 10 minutes. Press "match" to match zone 2 settings to zone 1. Press "start/stop" to begin.

Nutrition Info:

- (Per serving) Calories 203 | Fat 9g |Sodium 99mg | Carbs 0.9g | Fiber 0.2g | Sugar 0.2g | Protein 32.1g

Fish Sandwich

Servings: 4 | Cooking Time: 22 Minutes.

Ingredients:

- 4 small cod fillets, skinless
- Salt and black pepper, to taste
- 2 tablespoons flour
- ¼ cup dried breadcrumbs
- Spray oil
- 9 ounces of frozen peas
- 1 tablespoon creme fraiche
- 12 capers
- 1 squeeze of lemon juice
- 4 bread rolls, cut in halve

Directions:

1. First, coat the cod fillets with flour, salt, and black pepper.
2. Then coat the fish with breadcrumbs.
3. Divide the coated codfish in the two crisper plates and spray them with cooking spray.
4. Return the crisper plate to the Ninja Foodi Dual Zone Air Fryer.
5. Choose the Air Fry mode for Zone 1 and set the temperature to 390 degrees F and the time to 17 minutes.
6. Select the "MATCH" button to copy the settings for Zone 2.
7. Initiate cooking by pressing the START/STOP button.
8. Meanwhile, boil peas in hot water for 5 minutes until soft.
9. Then drain the peas and transfer them to the blender.
10. Add capers, lemon juice, and crème fraiche to the blender.
11. Blend until it makes a smooth mixture.
12. Spread the peas crème mixture on top of 2 lower halves of the bread roll, and place the fish fillets on it.
13. Place the remaining bread slices on top.
14. Serve fresh.

Nutrition Info:

- (Per serving) Calories 348 | Fat 30g |Sodium 660mg | Carbs 5g | Fiber 0g | Sugar 0g | Protein 14g

Fish And Chips

Servings:2 | Cooking Time:22

Ingredients:

- 1 pound of potatoes, cut lengthwise
- 1 cup seasoned flour
- 2 eggs, organic
- 1/3 cup buttermilk
- 2 cup seafood fry mix
- ½ cup bread crumbs
- 2 codfish fillet, 6 ounces each
- Oil spray, for greasing

Directions:

1. take a bowl and whisk eggs in it along buttermilk.
2. In a separate bowl mix seafood fry mix and bread crumbs
3. Take a baking tray and spread flour on it
4. Dip the fillets first in egg wash, then in flour, and at the end coat it with breadcrumbs mixture.
5. Put the fish fillet in air fryer zone 1 basket.
6. Grease the fish fillet with oil spray.
7. Set zone 1 to AIR FRY mode at 400 degrees F for 14 minutes.
8. Put potato chip in zone two baskets and lightly grease it with oil spray.
9. Set the zone 2 basket to AIRFRY mode at 400 degrees F for 22 minutes.
10. Hit the smart finish button.
11. Once done, serve and enjoy.

Nutrition Info:

- (Per serving) Calories 992| Fat 22.3g| Sodium1406 mg | Carbs 153.6g | Fiber 10g | Sugar10 g | Protein 40g

Salmon With Coconut

Servings:2 | Cooking Time:15

Ingredients:

- Oil spray, for greasing
- 2 salmon fillets, 6ounces each
- Salt and ground black pepper, to taste
- 1 tablespoon butter, for frying
- 1 tablespoon red curry paste
- 1 cup of coconut cream
- 2 tablespoons fresh cilantro, chopped
- 1 cup of cauliflower florets
- ½ cup Parmesan cheese, hard

Directions:

1. Take a bowl and mix salt, black pepper, butter, red curry paste, coconut cream in a bowl and marinate the salmon in it.
2. Oil sprays the cauliflower florets and then seasons it with salt and freshly ground black pepper.
3. Put the florets in the zone 1 basket.
4. Layer the parchment paper over the zone 2 baskets, and then place the salmon fillet on it.
5. Set the zone 2 basket to AIR FRY mod at 15 minutes for4 00 degrees F
6. Hit the smart finish button to finish it at the same time.
7. Once the time for cooking is over, serve the salmon with cauliflower floret with Parmesan cheese drizzle on top.

Nutrition Info:

- (Per serving) Calories 774 | Fat 59g| Sodium 1223mg | Carbs 12.2g | Fiber 3.9g | Sugar5.9 g | Protein53.5 g

Roasted Salmon And Parmesan Asparagus

Servings: 4 | Cooking Time: 27 Minutes

Ingredients:

- 2 tablespoons Montreal steak seasoning
- 3 tablespoons brown sugar
- 3 uncooked salmon fillets (6 ounces each)
- 2 tablespoons canola oil, divided
- 1-pound asparagus, ends trimmed
- Kosher salt, as desired
- Ground black pepper, as desired
- ¼ cup shredded parmesan cheese, divided

Directions:

1. Combine the steak spice and brown sugar in a small bowl.
2. Brush 1 tablespoon of oil over the salmon fillets, then thoroughly coat with the sugar mixture.
3. Toss the asparagus with the remaining 1 tablespoon of oil, salt, and pepper in a mixing bowl.
4. Place a crisper plate in both drawers. Put the fillets skin-side down in the zone 1 drawer, then place the drawer in the unit. Insert the zone 2 drawer into the device after placing the asparagus in it.
5. Select zone 1, then ROAST, then set the temperature to 390 degrees F/ 200 degrees C with a 17-minute timer. To match the zone 2 settings to zone 1, choose MATCH. To begin cooking, press the START/STOP button.
6. When the zone 2 timer reaches 7 minutes, press START/STOP. Remove the zone 2 drawer from the unit. Flip the asparagus with silicone-tipped tongs. Re-insert the drawer into the unit. Continue cooking by pressing START/STOP.
7. When the zone 2 timer has reached 14 minutes, press START/STOP. Remove the zone 2 drawer from the unit. Sprinkle half the parmesan cheese over the asparagus, and mix lightly. Re-insert the drawer into the unit. Continue cooking by pressing START/STOP.
8. Transfer the fillets and asparagus to a serving plate once they've finished cooking. Serve with the remaining parmesan cheese on top of the asparagus.

Nutrition Info:

- (Per serving) Calories 293 | Fat 15.8g | Sodium 203mg | Carbs 11.1g | Fiber 2.4g | Sugar 8.7g | Protein 29g

Pretzel-crusted Catfish

Servings: 4 | Cooking Time: 12 Minutes

Ingredients:

- 4 catfish fillets
- ½ teaspoon salt
- ½ teaspoon black pepper
- 2 large eggs
- ⅓ cup Dijon mustard
- 2 tablespoons 2% milk
- ½ cup all-purpose flour
- 4 cups miniature pretzels, crushed
- Cooking spray
- Lemon slices

Directions:

1. Rub the catfish with black pepper and salt.
2. Beat eggs with milk and mustard in a bowl.
3. Spread pretzels and flour in two separate bowls.
4. Coat the catfish with flour then dip in the egg mixture and coat with the pretzels.
5. Place two fish fillets in each air fryer basket.
6. Return the air fryer basket 1 to Zone 1, and basket 2 to Zone 2 of the Ninja Foodi 2-Basket Air Fryer.
7. Choose the "Air Fry" mode for Zone 1 at 325 degrees F and 12 minutes of cooking time.
8. Select the "MATCH COOK" option to copy the settings for Zone 2.
9. Initiate cooking by pressing the START/PAUSE BUT-

TON.
10. Serve warm.

Nutrition Info:

• (Per serving) Calories 196 | Fat 7.1g |Sodium 492mg | Carbs 21.6g | Fiber 2.9g | Sugar 0.8g | Protein 13.4g

Furikake Salmon

Servings: 4 | Cooking Time: 10 Minutes

Ingredients:

• ½ cup mayonnaise
• 1 tablespoon shoyu
• 455gsalmon fillet
• Salt and black pepper to taste
• 2 tablespoons furikake

Directions:

1. Mix shoyu with mayonnaise in a small bowl.
2. Rub the salmon with black pepper and salt.
3. Place the salmon pieces in the air fryer baskets.
4. Top them with the mayo mixture.
5. Return the air fryer basket 1 to Zone 1, and basket 2 to Zone 2 of the Ninja Foodi 2-Basket Air Fryer.
6. Choose the "Air Fry" mode for Zone 1 at 400 degrees F and 10 minutes of cooking time.
7. Select the "MATCH COOK" option to copy the settings for Zone 2.
8. Initiate cooking by pressing the START/PAUSE BUTTON.
9. Serve warm.

Nutrition Info:

• (Per serving) Calories 297 | Fat 1g |Sodium 291mg | Carbs 35g | Fiber 1g | Sugar 9g | Protein 29g

Smoked Salmon

Servings:4 | Cooking Time:12

Ingredients:

• 2 pounds of salmon fillets, smoked
• 6 ounces cream cheese
• 4 tablespoons mayonnaise
• 2 teaspoons of chives, fresh
• 1 teaspoon of lemon zest
• Salt and freshly ground black pepper, to taste
• 2 tablespoons of butter

Directions:

1. Cut the salmon into very small and uniform bite-size pieces.
2. Mix cream cheese, chives, mayonnaise, black pepper, and lemon zest, in a small mixing bowl.
3. Let it sit aside for further use.
4. Coat the salmon pieces with salt and butter.
5. Divide the bite-size pieces into both zones of the air fryer.
6. Set it on AIRFRY mode at 400 degrees F for 12 minutes.
7. Select MATCH for zone 2 basket.
8. Hit start, so the cooking start.
9. Once the salmon is done, top it with a bowl creamy mixture and serve.
10. Enjoy hot.

Nutrition Info:

• (Per serving) Calories 557| Fat 15.7 g| Sodium 371mg | Carbs 4.8 g | Fiber 0g | Sugar 1.1g | Protein 48 g

Scallops

Servings: 4 | Cooking Time: 5 Minutes

Ingredients:

• ½ cup Italian breadcrumbs
• ½ teaspoon garlic powder
• ¼ teaspoon salt
• ½ teaspoon black pepper
• 2 tablespoons butter, melted
• 1 pound sea scallops, rinsed and pat dry

Directions:

1. Combine the breadcrumbs, garlic powder, salt, and pepper in a small bowl. Pour the melted butter into another shallow bowl.
2. Dredge each scallop in the melted butter, then roll it in the breadcrumb mixture until well covered.
3. Place a crisper plate in each drawer. Put the scallops in a single layer in each drawer. Insert the drawers into the unit.
4. Select zone 1, then AIR FRY, then set the temperature to 360 degrees F/ 180 degrees C with a 5-minute timer. To match zone 2 settings to zone 1, choose MATCH. To begin, select START/STOP.
5. Press START/STOP to pause the unit when the timer reaches 3 minutes. Remove the drawers. Use tongs to carefully flip the scallops over. To resume cooking, re-insert the drawers into the unit and press START/STOP.
6. Remove the scallops from the drawers after the timer has finished.

Nutrition Info:

• (Per serving) Calories 81 | Fat 6g | Sodium 145mg | Carbs 3g | Fiber 4g | Sugar 1g | Protein 3g

Frozen Breaded Fish Fillet

Servings:2 | Cooking Time:12

Ingredients:

- 4 Frozen Breaded Fish Fillet
- Oil spray, for greasing
- 1 cup mayonnaise

Directions:

1. Take the frozen fish fillets out of the bag and place them in both baskets of the air fryer.
2. Lightly grease it with oil spray.
3. Set the Zone 1 basket to 380 degrees F fo12 minutes.
4. Select the MATCH button for the zone 2 basket.
5. hit the start button to start cooking.
6. Once the cooking is done, serve the fish hot with mayonnaise.

Nutrition Info:

- (Per serving) Calories 921| Fat 61.5g| Sodium 1575mg | Carbs 69g | Fiber 2g | Sugar 9.5g | Protein 29.1g

Shrimp Skewers

Servings: 4 | Cooking Time: 10minutes

Ingredients:

- 453g shrimp
- 15ml lemon juice
- 15ml olive oil
- 1 tbsp old bay seasoning
- 1 tsp garlic, minced

Directions:

1. Toss shrimp with old bay seasoning, garlic, lemon juice, and olive oil in a bowl.
2. Thread shrimp onto the soaked skewers.
3. Insert a crisper plate in the Ninja Foodi air fryer baskets.
4. Place the shrimp skewers in both baskets.
5. Select zone 1, then select "air fry" mode and set the temperature to 390 degrees F for 10 minutes. Press "match" to match zone 2 settings to zone 1. Press "start/stop" to begin.

Nutrition Info:

- (Per serving) Calories 167 | Fat 5.5g |Sodium 758mg | Carbs 2g | Fiber 0g | Sugar 0.1g | Protein 25.9g

Chili Lime Tilapia

Servings: 4 | Cooking Time: 10 Minutes

Ingredients:

- 340g tilapia fillets
- 2 teaspoons chili powder
- 1 teaspoon cumin
- 1 teaspoon garlic powder
- ½ teaspoon oregano
- ½ teaspoon sea salt
- ¼ teaspoon black pepper
- Lime zest from 1 lime
- Juice of ½ lime

Directions:

1. Mix chili powder and other spices with lime juice and zest in a bowl.
2. Rub this spice mixture over the tilapia fillets.
3. Place two fillets in each air basket.
4. Return the air fryer basket to the Ninja Foodi 2 Baskets Air Fryer.
5. Choose the "Air Fry" mode for Zone 1 at 400 degrees F and 10 minutes of cooking time.
6. Select the "MATCH COOK" option to copy the settings for Zone 2.
7. Initiate cooking by pressing the START/PAUSE BUTTON.
8. Flip the tilapia fillets once cooked halfway through.
9. Serve warm.

Nutrition Info:

- (Per serving) Calories 275 | Fat 1.4g |Sodium 582mg | Carbs 31.5g | Fiber 1.1g | Sugar 0.1g | Protein 29.8g

Pecan-crusted Catfish Nuggets With "fried" Okra

Servings:4 | Cooking Time: 17 Minutes

Ingredients:

- FOR THE CATFISH NUGGETS
- 1 cup whole milk
- 1 pound fresh catfish nuggets (or cut-up fillets)
- 1 large egg
- 2 to 3 dashes Louisiana-style hot sauce (optional)
- ¼ cup finely chopped pecans
- ½ cup all-purpose flour
- Nonstick cooking spray
- Tartar sauce, for serving (optional)
- FOR THE OKRA
- ½ cup fine yellow cornmeal
- ¼ cup all-purpose flour
- ½ teaspoon garlic powder
- ½ teaspoon paprika
- 1 teaspoon kosher salt
- 1 large egg

- 8 ounces frozen cut okra, thawed
- Nonstick cooking spray

Directions:

1. To prep the catfish: Pour the milk into a large zip-top bag. Add the catfish and turn to coat. Set in the refrigerator to soak for at least 1 hour or up to overnight.
2. Remove the fish from the milk, shaking off any excess liquid.
3. In a shallow dish, whisk together the egg and hot sauce (if using). In a second shallow dish, combine the pecans and flour.
4. Dip each piece of fish into the egg mixture, then into the nut mixture to coat. Gently press the nut mixture to adhere to the fish. Spritz each nugget with cooking spray.
5. To prep the okra: Set up a breading station with two small shallow bowls. In the first bowl, stir together the cornmeal, flour, garlic powder, paprika, and salt. In the second bowl, whisk the egg.
6. Dip the okra first in the cornmeal mixture, then the egg, then back into the cornmeal. Spritz with cooking spray.
7. To cook the catfish and okra: Install a crisper plate in each of the two baskets. Place the fish in a single layer in the Zone 1 basket and insert the basket in the unit. Place the okra in the Zone 2 basket and insert the basket in the unit.
8. Select Zone 1, select AIR FRY, set the temperature to 390°F, and set the timer to 17 minutes.
9. Select Zone 2, select AIR FRY, set the temperature to 400°F, and set the timer to 12 minutes. Select SMART FINISH.
10. Press START/PAUSE to begin cooking.
11. When cooking is complete, the fish should be cooked through and the okra golden brown and crispy. Serve hot.

Nutrition Info:

- (Per serving) Calories: 414; Total fat: 24g; Saturated fat: 2.5g; Carbohydrates: 30g; Fiber: 3g; Protein: 23g; Sodium: 569mg

Lemon Pepper Salmon With Asparagus

Servings:2 | Cooking Time:18

Ingredients:

- 1 cup of green asparagus
- 2 tablespoons of butter
- 2 fillets of salmon, 8 ounces each
- Salt and black pepper, to taste
- 1 teaspoon of lemon juice
- ½ teaspoon of lemon zest
- oil spray, for greasing

Directions:

1. Rinse and trim the asparagus.
2. Rinse and pat dry the salmon fillets.
3. Take a bowl and mix lemon juice, lemon zest, salt, and black pepper.
4. Brush the fish fillet with the rub and place it in the zone 1 basket.
5. Place asparagus in zone 2 basket.
6. Spray the asparagus with oil spray.
7. Set zone 1 to AIRFRY mode for 18 minutes at 390 degrees F.
8. Set the zone 2 to 5 minutes at 390 degrees F, at air fry mode.
9. Hit the smart finish button to finish at the same time.
10. Once done, serve and enjoy.

Nutrition Info:

- (Per serving) Calories 482| Fat 28g| Sodium209 mg | Carbs 2.8g | Fiber1.5 g | Sugar1.4 g | Protein 56.3g

Fried Lobster Tails

Servings: 4 | Cooking Time: 18 Minutes.

Ingredients:

- 4 (4-oz) lobster tails
- 8 tablespoons butter, melted
- 2 teaspoons lemon zest
- 2 garlic cloves, grated
- Salt and black pepper, ground to taste
- 2 teaspoons fresh parsley, chopped
- 4 wedges lemon

Directions:

1. Spread the lobster tails into Butterfly, slit the top to expose the lobster meat while keeping the tail intact.
2. Place two lobster tails in each of the crisper plate with their lobster meat facing up.
3. Mix melted butter with lemon zest and garlic in a bowl.
4. Brush the butter mixture on top of the lobster tails.
5. And drizzle salt and black pepper on top.
6. Return the crisper plate to the Ninja Foodi Dual Zone Air Fryer.
7. Choose the Air Fry mode for Zone 1 and set the temperature to 390 degrees F and the time to 18 minutes.
8. Select the "MATCH" button to copy the settings for Zone 2.
9. Initiate cooking by pressing the START/STOP button.
10. Garnish with parsley and lemon wedges.
11. Serve warm.

Nutrition Info:

- (Per serving) Calories 257 | Fat 10.4g |Sodium 431mg | Carbs 20g | Fiber 0g | Sugar 1.6g | Protein 21g

Savory Salmon Fillets

Servings: 4 | Cooking Time: 17 Minutes.

Ingredients:

- 4 (6-oz) salmon fillets
- Salt, to taste
- Black pepper, to taste
- 4 teaspoons olive oil
- 4 tablespoons wholegrain mustard
- 2 tablespoons packed brown sugar
- 2 garlic cloves, minced
- 1 teaspoon thyme leaves

Directions:

1. Rub the salmon with salt and black pepper first.
2. Whisk oil with sugar, thyme, garlic, and mustard in a small bowl.
3. Place two salmon fillets in each of the crisper plate and brush the thyme mixture on top of each fillet.
4. Return the crisper plates to the Ninja Foodi Dual Zone Air Fryer.
5. Choose the Air Fry mode for Zone 1 and set the temperature to 390 degrees F and the time to 17 minutes.
6. Select the "MATCH" button to copy the settings for Zone 2.
7. Initiate cooking by pressing the START/STOP button.
8. Serve warm and fresh.

Nutrition Info:

- (Per serving) Calories 336 | Fat 6g |Sodium 181mg | Carbs 1.3g | Fiber 0.2g | Sugar 0.4g | Protein 69.2g

Tasty Parmesan Shrimp

Servings: 6 | Cooking Time: 10minutes

Ingredients:

- 908g cooked shrimp, peeled & deveined
- ½ tsp oregano
- 59g parmesan cheese, grated
- 1 tbsp garlic, minced
- 30ml olive oil
- 1 tsp onion powder
- 1 tsp basil
- Pepper
- Salt

Directions:

1. Toss shrimp with oregano, cheese, garlic, oil, onion powder, basil, pepper, and salt in a bowl.
2. Insert a crisper plate in the Ninja Foodi air fryer baskets.
3. Add the shrimp mixture to both baskets.
4. Select zone 1, then select "air fry" mode and set the temperature to 360 degrees F for 10 minutes. Press "match" to match zone 2 settings to zone 1. Press "start/stop" to begin.

Nutrition Info:

- (Per serving) Calories 224 | Fat 7.3g |Sodium 397mg | Carbs 3.2g | Fiber 0.1g | Sugar 0.2g | Protein 34.6g

Keto Baked Salmon With Pesto

Servings:2 | Cooking Time:18

Ingredients:

- 4 salmon fillets, 2 inches thick
- 2 ounces green pesto
- Salt and black pepper
- ½ tablespoon of canola oil, for greasing
- 1-1/2 cup mayonnaise
- 2 tablespoons Greek yogurt
- Salt and black pepper, to taste

Directions:

1. Rub the salmon with pesto, salt, oil, and black pepper.
2. In a small bowl, whisk together all the green sauce ingredients.
3. Divide the fish fillets between both the baskets.
4. Set zone 1 to air fry mode for 18 minutes at 390 degrees F.
5. Select MATCH button for Zone 2 basket.
6. Once the cooking is done, serve it with green sauce drizzle.
7. Enjoy.

Nutrition Info:

- (Per serving) Calories 1165 | Fat80.7 g| Sodium 1087 mg | Carbs 33.1g | Fiber 0.5g | Sugar11.5 g | Protein 80.6g

Tuna Patties

Servings: 6 | Cooking Time: 10 Minutes

Ingredients:

- For the tuna patties:
- 1 tablespoon extra-virgin olive oil
- 1 tablespoon butter
- ½ cup chopped onion
- ½ red bell pepper, chopped
- 1 teaspoon minced garlic
- 2 (7-ounce) cans or 3 (5-ounce) cans albacore tuna fish in water, drained
- 1 tablespoon lime juice
- 1 celery stalk, chopped
- ¼ cup chopped fresh parsley
- 3 tablespoons grated parmesan cheese
- ½ teaspoon dried oregano
- ¼ teaspoon salt
- Black pepper, to taste
- 1 teaspoon sriracha
- ½ cup panko crumbs
- 2 whisked eggs

- For the crumb coating:
- ½ cup panko crumbs
- ¼ cup parmesan cheese
- Non-stick spray

Directions:

1. In a skillet, heat the oil and butter over medium-high heat.
2. Sauté the onions, red bell pepper, and garlic for 5 to 7 minutes.
3. Drain the tuna from the cans thoroughly. Put the tuna in a large mixing bowl. Add the lime juice.
4. Add the sautéed vegetables to the mixing bowl.
5. Add the celery, parsley, and cheese. Combine well.
6. Add the oregano, salt, and pepper to taste. Mix well.
7. Add a dash of sriracha for a spicy kick and mix well.
8. Add the panko crumbs and mix well.
9. Mix in the eggs until the mixture is well combined. You can add an extra egg if necessary, but the tuna is usually wet enough that it isn't required. Form 6 patties from the mixture.
10. Refrigerate for 30 to 60 minutes (or even overnight).
11. Remove from refrigerator and coat with a mixture of the ½ cup of panko crumbs and ¼ cup of parmesan cheese.
12. Spray the tops of the coated patties with some non-stick cooking spray.
13. Place a crisper place in each drawer. Put 3 patties in each drawer. Insert the drawers into the unit.
14. Select zone 1, then AIR FRY, then set the temperature to 390 degrees F/ 200 degrees C with a 10-minute timer. To match zone 2 settings to zone 1, choose MATCH. To begin, select START/STOP.
15. Remove and garnish with chopped parsley.

Nutrition Info:

- (Per serving) Calories 381 | Fat 16g | Sodium 1007mg | Carbs 23g | Fiber 2g | Sugar 4g | Protein 38g

Blackened Mahimahi With Honey-roasted Carrots

Servings:4 | Cooking Time: 30 Minutes

Ingredients:

- FOR THE MAHIMAHI
- 4 mahimahi fillets (4 ounces each)
- 1 tablespoon olive oil
- 1 tablespoon blackening seasoning
- Lemon wedges, for serving
- FOR THE CARROTS
- 1 pound carrots, peeled and cut into ½-inch rounds
- 2 teaspoons vegetable oil
- ½ teaspoon kosher salt
- ¼ teaspoon freshly ground black pepper
- 1 tablespoon salted butter, cut into small pieces
- 1 tablespoon honey
- 2 tablespoons chopped fresh parsley

Directions:

1. To prep the mahimahi: Brush both sides of the fish with the oil and sprinkle with the blackening seasoning.
2. To prep the carrots: In a large bowl, combine the carrots, oil, salt, and black pepper. Stir well to coat the carrots with the oil.
3. To cook the mahimahi and carrots: Install a crisper plate in each of the two baskets. Place the fish in the Zone 1 basket and insert the basket in the unit. Place the carrots in the Zone 2 basket and insert the basket in the unit.
4. Select Zone 1, select AIR FRY, set the temperature to 380°F, and set the timer to 14 minutes.
5. Select Zone 2, select ROAST, set the temperature to 400°F, and set the timer to 30 minutes. Select SMART FINISH.
6. Press START/PAUSE to begin cooking.
7. When the Zone 2 timer reads 15 minutes, press START/PAUSE. Remove the basket and scatter the butter over the carrots, then drizzle them with the honey. Reinsert the basket and press START/PAUSE to resume cooking.
8. When cooking is complete, the fish should be cooked through and the carrots soft.
9. Stir the parsley into the carrots. Serve the fish with lemon wedges.

Nutrition Info:

- (Per serving) Calories: 235; Total fat: 9.5g; Saturated fat: 3g; Carbohydrates: 15g; Fiber: 3g; Protein: 22g; Sodium: 672mg

Vegetables And Sides Recipes

Green Salad With Crispy Fried Goat Cheese And Baked Croutons

Servings:4 | Cooking Time: 10 Minutes

Ingredients:

- FOR THE GOAT CHEESE
- 1 (4-ounce) log soft goat cheese
- ½ cup panko bread crumbs
- 2 tablespoons vegetable oil
- FOR THE CROUTONS
- 2 slices Italian-style sandwich bread
- 2 tablespoons vegetable oil
- 1 tablespoon poultry seasoning
- ½ teaspoon kosher salt
- ¼ teaspoon freshly ground black pepper
- FOR THE SALAD
- 8 cups green leaf lettuce leaves
- ½ cup store-bought balsamic vinaigrette

Directions:

1. To prep the goat cheese: Cut the goat cheese into 8 round slices.
2. Spread the panko on a plate. Gently press the cheese into the panko to coat on both sides. Drizzle with the oil.
3. To prep the croutons: Cut the bread into cubes and place them in a large bowl. Add the oil, poultry seasoning, salt, and black pepper. Mix well to coat the bread cubes evenly.
4. To cook the goat cheese and croutons: Install a crisper plate in each of the two baskets. Place the goat cheese in the Zone 1 basket and insert the basket in the unit. Place the croutons in the Zone 2 basket and insert the basket in the unit.
5. Select Zone 1, select AIR FRY, set the temperature to 400°F, and set the timer to 6 minutes.
6. Select Zone 2, select BAKE, set the temperature to 390°F, and set the timer to 10 minutes. Select SMART FINISH.
7. Press START/PAUSE to begin cooking.
8. When cooking is complete, the goat cheese will be golden brown and the croutons crisp.
9. Remove the Zone 1 basket. Let the goat cheese cool in the basket for 5 minutes; it will firm up as it cools.
10. To assemble the salad: In a large bowl, combine the lettuce, vinaigrette, and croutons. Toss well. Divide the salad among four plates. Top each plate with 2 pieces of goat cheese.

Nutrition Info:

- (Per serving) Calories: 578; Total fat: 40g; Saturated fat: 14g; Carbohydrates: 39g; Fiber: 3.5g; Protein: 24g; Sodium: 815mg

Balsamic Vegetables

Servings: 4 | Cooking Time: 13 Minutes

Ingredients:

- 125g asparagus, cut woody ends
- 88g mushrooms, halved
- 1 tbsp Dijon mustard
- 3 tbsp soy sauce
- 27g brown sugar
- 57ml balsamic vinegar
- 32g olive oil
- 1 zucchini, sliced
- 1 yellow squash, sliced
- 170g grape tomatoes
- Pepper
- Salt

Directions:

1. In a bowl, mix asparagus, tomatoes, oil, mustard, soy sauce, mushrooms, zucchini, squash, brown sugar, vinegar, pepper, and salt.
2. Cover the bowl and place it in the refrigerator for 45 minutes.
3. Insert a crisper plate in the Ninja Foodi air fryer baskets.
4. Add the vegetable mixture in both baskets.
5. Select zone 1, then select "air fry" mode and set the temperature to 390 degrees F for 12 minutes. Press "match" to match zone 2 settings to zone 1. Press "start/stop" to begin. Stir halfway through.

Nutrition Info:

- (Per serving) Calories 184 | Fat 13.3g |Sodium 778mg | Carbs 14.7g | Fiber 3.6g | Sugar 9.5g | Protein 5.5g

Fried Artichoke Hearts

Servings: 6 | Cooking Time: 10 Minutes.

Ingredients:

- 3 cans Quartered Artichokes, drained
- ½ cup mayonnaise
- 1 cup panko breadcrumbs
- ⅓ cup grated Parmesan
- salt and black pepper to taste
- Parsley for garnish

Directions:

1. Mix mayonnaise with salt and black pepper and keep the sauce aside.
2. Spread panko breadcrumbs in a bowl.
3. Coat the artichoke pieces with the breadcrumbs.
4. As you coat the artichokes, place them in the two crisper plates in a single layer, then spray them with cooking oil.
5. Return the crisper plates to the Ninja Foodi Dual Zone Air Fryer.
6. Choose the Air Fry mode for Zone 1 and set the temperature to 375 degrees F and the time to 10 minutes.
7. Select the "MATCH" button to copy the settings for Zone 2.
8. Initiate cooking by pressing the START/STOP button.
9. Flip the artichokes once cooked halfway through, then resume cooking.
10. Serve warm with mayo sauce.

Nutrition Info:

- (Per serving) Calories 193 | Fat 1g |Sodium 395mg | Carbs 38.7g | Fiber 1.6g | Sugar 0.9g | Protein 6.6g

Zucchini Cakes

Servings: 6 | Cooking Time: 32 Minutes.

Ingredients:

- 2 medium zucchinis, grated
- 1 cup corn kernel
- 1 medium potato cooked
- 2 tablespoons chickpea flour
- 2 garlic minced
- 2 teaspoons olive oil
- Salt and black pepper
- For Serving:
- Yogurt tahini sauce

Directions:

1. Mix grated zucchini with a pinch of salt in a colander and leave them for 15 minutes.
2. Squeeze out their excess water.
3. Mash the cooked potato in a large-sized bowl with a fork.
4. Add zucchini, corn, garlic, chickpea flour, salt, and black pepper to the bowl.
5. Mix these fritters' ingredients together and make 2 tablespoons-sized balls out of this mixture and flatten them lightly.
6. Divide the fritters in the two crisper plates in a single layer and spray them with cooking.
7. Return the crisper plates to the Ninja Foodi Dual Zone Air Fryer.
8. Choose the Air Fry mode for Zone 1 and set the temperature to 390 degrees F and the time to 17 minutes.
9. Select the "MATCH" button to copy the settings for Zone 2.
10. Initiate cooking by pressing the START/STOP button.
11. Flip the fritters once cooked halfway through, then resume cooking.
12. Serve.

Nutrition Info:

- (Per serving) Calories 270 | Fat 14.6g |Sodium 394mg | Carbs 31.3g | Fiber 7.5g | Sugar 9.7g | Protein 6.4g

Garlic Potato Wedges In Air Fryer

Servings:2 | Cooking Time:23

Ingredients:

- 4 medium potatoes, peeled and cut into wedges
- 4 tablespoons of butter
- 1 teaspoon of chopped cilantro
- 1 cup plain flour
- 1 teaspoon of garlic, minced
- Salt and black pepper, to taste

Directions:

1. Soak the potatoes wedges in cold water for about 30 minutes.
2. Then drain and pat dry with a paper towel.
3. Boil water in a large pot and boil the wedges just for 3 minutes.
4. Then take it out on a paper towel.
5. Now in a bowl mix garlic, melted butter, salt, pepper, cilantro and whisk it well.
6. Add the flour to a separate bowl and add salt and black pepper.
7. Then add water to the flour so it gets runny in texture.
8. Now, coat the potatoes with flour mixture and add it to two foil tins.
9. Put foil tins in both the air fryer basket.
10. Now, set time for zone 1 basket using AIRFRY mode at 390 degrees F for 20 minutes.
11. Select the MATCH button for the zone 2 basket.
12. Once done, serve and enjoy.

Nutrition Info:

- (Per serving) Calories 727| Fat 24.1g| Sodium 191mg | Carbs 115.1g | Fiber 12g | Sugar 5.1g | Protein14 g

Pepper Poppers

Servings: 24 | Cooking Time: 20 Minutes

Ingredients:

- 8 ounces cream cheese, softened
- ¾ cup shredded cheddar cheese
- ¾ cup shredded Monterey Jack cheese
- 6 bacon strips, cooked and crumbled
- ¼ teaspoon salt
- ¼ teaspoon garlic powder
- ¼ teaspoon chili powder
- ¼ teaspoon smoked paprika
- 1-pound fresh jalapeño peppers, halved lengthwise and deseeded
- ½ cup dry breadcrumbs
- Sour cream, French onion dip, or ranch salad dressing (optional)

Directions:

1. In a large bowl, combine the cheeses, bacon, and seasonings; mix well. Spoon 1½ to 2 tablespoons of the mixture into each pepper half. Roll them in the breadcrumbs.
2. Place a crisper plate in each drawer. Put the prepared peppers in a single layer in each drawer. Insert the drawers into the unit.
3. Select zone 1, then AIR FRY, then set the temperature to 360 degrees F/ 180 degrees C with a 20-minute timer. To match zone 2 settings to zone 1, choose MATCH. To begin, select START/STOP.
4. Remove the peppers from the drawers after the timer has finished.

Nutrition Info:

- (Per serving) Calories 81 | Fat 6g | Sodium 145mg | Carbs 3g | Fiber 4g | Sugar 1g | Protein 3g

Hasselback Potatoes

Servings: 4 | Cooking Time: 15 Minutes.

Ingredients:

- 4 medium Yukon Gold potatoes
- 3 tablespoons melted butter
- 1 tablespoon olive oil
- 3 garlic cloves, crushed
- ½ teaspoon ground paprika
- Salt and black pepper ground, to taste
- 1 tablespoon chopped fresh parsley

Directions:

1. Slice each potato from the top to make ¼-inch slices without cutting its ½-inch bottom, keeping the potato's bottom intact.
2. Mix butter with olive oil, garlic, and paprika in a small bowl.
3. Brush the garlic mixture on top of each potato and add the mixture into the slits.
4. Season them with salt and black pepper.
5. Place 2 seasoned potatoes in each of the crisper plate
6. Return the crisper plate to the Ninja Foodi Dual Zone Air Fryer.
7. Choose the Air Fry mode for Zone 1 and set the temperature to 375 degrees F and the time to 25 minutes.
8. Select the "MATCH" button to copy the settings for Zone 2.
9. Initiate cooking by pressing the START/STOP button.
10. Brushing the potatoes again with butter mixture after 15 minutes, then resume cooking.
11. Garnish with parsley.
12. Serve warm.

Nutrition Info:

- (Per serving) Calories 350 | Fat 2.6g |Sodium 358mg | Carbs 64.6g | Fiber 14.4g | Sugar 3.3g | Protein 19.9g

Potatoes & Beans

Servings: 4 | Cooking Time: 25 Minutes

Ingredients:

- 453g potatoes, cut into pieces
- 15ml olive oil
- 1 tsp garlic powder
- 160g green beans, trimmed
- Pepper
- Salt

Directions:

1. In a bowl, toss green beans, garlic powder, potatoes, oil, pepper, and salt.
2. Insert a crisper plate in the Ninja Foodi air fryer baskets.
3. Add green beans and potato mixture to both baskets.
4. Select zone 1 then select "air fry" mode and set the temperature to 380 degrees F for 25 minutes. Press "match" to match zone 2 settings to zone 1. Press "start/stop" to begin. Stir halfway through.

Nutrition Info:

- (Per serving) Calories 128 | Fat 3.7g |Sodium 49mg | Carbs 22.4g | Fiber 4.7g | Sugar 2.3g | Protein 3.1g

Broccoli, Squash, & Pepper

Servings: 4 | Cooking Time: 12 Minutes

Ingredients:

- 175g broccoli florets
- 1 red bell pepper, diced
- 1 tbsp olive oil
- ½ tsp garlic powder
- ¼ onion, sliced
- 1 zucchini, sliced
- 2 yellow squash, sliced

- Pepper
- Salt

Directions:

1. In a bowl, toss veggies with oil, garlic powder, pepper, and salt.
2. Insert a crisper plate in the Ninja Foodi air fryer baskets.
3. Add the vegetable mixture in both baskets.
4. Select zone 1 then select "air fry" mode and set the temperature to 390 degrees F for 12 minutes. Press "match" to match zone 2 settings to zone 1. Press "start/stop" to begin. Stir halfway through.

Nutrition Info:

- (Per serving) Calories 75 | Fat 3.9g |Sodium 62mg | Carbs 9.6g | Fiber 2.8g | Sugar 4.8g | Protein 2.9g

Falafel

Servings: 6 | Cooking Time: 14 Minutes.

Ingredients:

- 1 (15.5-oz) can chickpeas, rinsed and drained
- 1 small yellow onion, cut into quarters
- 3 garlic cloves, chopped
- ⅓ cup parsley, chopped
- ⅓ cup cilantro, chopped
- ⅓ cup scallions, chopped
- 1 teaspoon cumin
- ½ teaspoons salt
- ⅛ teaspoons crushed red pepper flakes
- 1 teaspoon baking powder
- 4 tablespoons all-purpose flour
- Olive oil spray

Directions:

1. Dry the chickpeas on paper towels.
2. Add onions and garlic to a food processor and chop them.
3. Add the parsley, salt, cilantro, scallions, cumin, and red pepper flakes.
4. Press the pulse button for 60 seconds, then toss in chickpeas and blend for 3 times until it makes a chunky paste.
5. Stir in baking powder and flour and mix well.
6. Transfer the falafel mixture to a bowl and cover to refrigerate for 3 hours.
7. Make 12 balls out of the falafel mixture.
8. Place 6 falafels in each of the crisper plate and spray them with oil.
9. Return the crisper plate to the Ninja Foodi Dual Zone Air Fryer.
10. Choose the Air Fry mode for Zone 1 and set the temperature to 350 degrees F and the time to 14 minutes.
11. Select the "MATCH" button to copy the settings for Zone 2.
12. Initiate cooking by pressing the START/STOP button.
13. Toss the falafel once cooked halfway through, and resume cooking.
14. Serve warm.

Nutrition Info:

- (Per serving) Calories 113 | Fat 3g |Sodium 152mg | Carbs 20g | Fiber 3g | Sugar 1.1g | Protein 3.5g

Buffalo Seitan With Crispy Zucchini Noodles

Servings:4 | Cooking Time: 12 Minutes

Ingredients:

- FOR THE BUFFALO SEITAN
- 1 (8-ounce) package precooked seitan strips
- 1 teaspoon garlic powder, divided
- ½ teaspoon onion powder
- ¼ teaspoon smoked paprika
- ¼ cup Louisiana-style hot sauce
- 2 tablespoons vegetable oil
- 1 tablespoon tomato paste
- ¼ teaspoon freshly ground black pepper
- FOR THE ZUCCHINI NOODLES
- 3 large egg whites
- 1¼ cups all-purpose flour
- 1 teaspoon kosher salt, divided
- 12 ounces seltzer water or club soda
- 5 ounces zucchini noodles
- Nonstick cooking spray

Directions:

1. To prep the Buffalo seitan: Season the seitan strips with ½ teaspoon of garlic powder, the onion powder, and smoked paprika.
2. In a large bowl, whisk together the hot sauce, oil, tomato paste, remaining ½ teaspoon of garlic powder, and the black pepper. Set the bowl of Buffalo sauce aside.
3. To prep the zucchini noodles: In a medium bowl, use a handheld mixer to beat the egg whites until stiff peaks form.
4. In a large bowl, combine the flour and ½ teaspoon of salt. Mix in the seltzer to form a thin batter. Fold in the beaten egg whites.
5. Add the zucchini to the batter and gently mix to coat.
6. To cook the seitan and zucchini noodles: Install a crisper plate in each of the two baskets. Place the seitan in the Zone 1 basket and insert the basket in the unit. Lift the noodles from the batter one at a time, letting the excess drip off, and place them in the Zone 2 basket. Insert the basket in the unit.
7. Select Zone 1, select BAKE, set the temperature to 370°F, and set the timer to 12 minutes.

8. Select Zone 2, select AIR FRY, set the temperature to 400°F, and set the timer to 12 minutes. Select SMART FINISH.
9. Press START/PAUSE to begin cooking.
10. When the Zone 1 timer reads 2 minutes, press START/PAUSE. Remove the basket and transfer the seitan to the bowl of Buffalo sauce. Turn to coat, then return the seitan to the basket. Reinsert the basket and press START/PAUSE to resume cooking.
11. When cooking is complete, the seitan should be warmed through and the zucchini noodles crisp and light golden brown.
12. Sprinkle the zucchini noodles with the remaining ½ teaspoon of salt. If desired, drizzle extra Buffalo sauce over the seitan. Serve hot.

Nutrition Info:

- (Per serving) Calories: 252; Total fat: 15g; Saturated fat: 1g; Carbohydrates: 22g; Fiber: 1.5g; Protein: 13g; Sodium: 740mg

Jerk Tofu With Roasted Cabbage

Servings:4 | Cooking Time: 20 Minutes

Ingredients:

- FOR THE JERK TOFU
- 1 (14-ounce) package extra-firm tofu, drained
- 1 tablespoon apple cider vinegar
- 1 tablespoon reduced-sodium soy sauce
- 2 tablespoons jerk seasoning
- Juice of 1 lime
- ½ teaspoon kosher salt
- 2 tablespoons olive oil
- FOR THE CABBAGE
- 1 (14-ounce) bag coleslaw mix
- 1 red bell pepper, thinly sliced
- 2 scallions, thinly sliced
- 2 tablespoons water
- 3 garlic cloves, minced
- ¼ teaspoon fresh thyme leaves
- ¼ teaspoon onion powder
- ¼ teaspoon kosher salt
- ¼ teaspoon freshly ground black pepper

Directions:

1. To prep the jerk tofu: Cut the tofu horizontally into 4 slabs.
2. In a shallow dish (big enough to hold the tofu slabs), whisk together the vinegar, soy sauce, jerk seasoning, lime juice, and salt.
3. Place the tofu in the marinade and turn to coat both sides. Cover and marinate for at least 15 minutes (or up to overnight in the refrigerator).
4. To prep the cabbage: In the Zone 2 basket, combine the coleslaw, bell pepper, scallions, water, garlic, thyme, onion powder, salt, and black pepper.
5. To cook the tofu and cabbage: Install a crisper plate in the Zone 1 basket and add the tofu in a single layer. Brush the tofu with the oil and insert the basket in the unit. Insert the Zone 2 basket in the unit.
6. Select Zone 1, select AIR FRY, set the temperature to 390°F, and set the timer to 15 minutes.
7. Select Zone 2, select ROAST, set the temperature to 330°F, and set the timer to 20 minutes. Select SMART FINISH.
8. Press START/PAUSE to begin cooking.
9. When both timers read 5 minutes, press START/PAUSE. Remove the Zone 1 basket and use silicone-tipped tongs to flip the tofu. Reinsert the basket in the unit. Remove the Zone 2 basket and stir the cabbage. Reinsert the basket and press START/PAUSE to resume cooking.
10. When cooking is complete, the tofu will be crispy and browned around the edges and the cabbage soft.
11. Transfer the tofu to four plates and serve with the cabbage on the side.

Nutrition Info:

- (Per serving) Calories: 220; Total fat: 12g; Saturated fat: 1.5g; Carbohydrates: 21g; Fiber: 5g; Protein: 12g; Sodium: 817mg

Fresh Mix Veggies In Air Fryer

Servings:4 | Cooking Time:12

Ingredients:

- 1 cup cauliflower florets
- 1 cup of carrots, peeled chopped
- 1 cup broccoli florets
- 2 tablespoons of avocado oil
- Salt, to taste
- ½ teaspoon of chili powder
- ½ teaspoon of garlic powder
- ½ teaspoon of herbs de Provence
- 1 cup parmesan cheese

Directions:

1. Take a bowl, and add all the veggies to it.
2. Toss and then season the veggies with salt, chili powder, garlic powder, and herbs de Provence.
3. Toss it all well and then drizzle avocado oil.
4. Make sure the ingredients are coated well.
5. Now distribute the veggies among both baskets of the air fryer.
6. Turn on the start button and set it to AIR FRY mode at 390 degrees for 10-12 minutes.
7. For the zone 2 basket setting, press the MATCH button.
8. After 8 minutes of cooking, select the pause button and then take out the baskets and sprinkle Parmesan

cheese on top of the veggies.

9. Then let the cooking cycle complete for the next 3-4 minutes.

10. Once done, serve.

Nutrition Info:

- (Per serving) Calories161 | Fat 9.3g| Sodium434 mg | Carbs 7.7g | Fiber 2.4g | Sugar 2.5g | Protein 13.9

Fried Olives

Servings: 6 | Cooking Time: 9 Minutes.

Ingredients:

- 2 cups blue cheese stuffed olives, drained
- ½ cup all-purpose flour
- 1 cup panko breadcrumbs
- ½ teaspoon garlic powder
- 1 pinch oregano
- 2 eggs

Directions:

1. Mix flour with oregano and garlic powder in a bowl and beat two eggs in another bowl.
2. Spread panko breadcrumbs in a bowl.
3. Coat all the olives with the flour mixture, dip in the eggs and then coat with the panko breadcrumbs.
4. As you coat the olives, place them in the two crisper plates in a single layer, then spray them with cooking oil.
5. Return the crisper plates to the Ninja Foodi Dual Zone Air Fryer.
6. Choose the Air Fry mode for Zone 1 and set the temperature to 375 degrees F and the time to 9 minutes.
7. Select the "MATCH" button to copy the settings for Zone 2.
8. Initiate cooking by pressing the START/STOP button.
9. Flip the olives once cooked halfway through, then resume cooking.
10. Serve.

Nutrition Info:

- (Per serving) Calories 166 | Fat 3.2g |Sodium 437mg | Carbs 28.8g | Fiber 1.8g | Sugar 2.7g | Protein 5.8g

Caprese Panini With Zucchini Chips

Servings:4 | Cooking Time: 20 Minutes

Ingredients:

- FOR THE PANINI
- 4 tablespoons pesto
- 8 slices Italian-style sandwich bread
- 1 tomato, diced
- 6 ounces fresh mozzarella cheese, shredded
- ¼ cup mayonnaise
- FOR THE ZUCCHINI CHIPS
- ½ cup all-purpose flour
- 2 large eggs
- ¼ teaspoon freshly ground black pepper
- ⅛ teaspoon kosher salt
- ½ cup panko bread crumbs
- ¼ cup grated Parmesan cheese
- 1 teaspoon Italian seasoning
- 1 medium zucchini, cut into ¼-inch-thick rounds
- 2 tablespoons vegetable oil

Directions:

1. To prep the panini: Spread 1 tablespoon of pesto each on 4 slices of the bread. Layer the diced tomato and shredded mozzarella on the other 4 slices of bread. Top the tomato/cheese mixture with the pesto-coated bread, pesto-side down, to form 4 sandwiches.
2. Spread the outside of each sandwich (both bread slices) with a thin layer of the mayonnaise.
3. To prep the zucchini chips: Set up a breading station with three small shallow bowls. Place the flour in the first bowl. In the second bowl, beat together the eggs, salt, and black pepper. Place the panko, Parmesan, and Italian seasoning in the third bowl.
4. Bread the zucchini in this order: First, dip the slices into the flour, coating both sides. Then, dip into the beaten egg. Finally, coat in the panko mixture. Drizzle the zucchini on both sides with the oil.
5. To cook the panini and zucchini chips: Install a crisper plate in each of the two baskets. Place 2 sandwiches in the Zone 1 basket and insert the basket in the unit. Place half of the zucchini chips in a single layer in the Zone 2 basket and insert the basket in the unit.
6. Select Zone 1, select AIR FRY, set the temperature to 375°F, and set the timer to 20 minutes.
7. Select Zone 2, select AIR FRY, set the temperature to 400°F, and set the timer to 20 minutes. Select SMART FINISH.
8. Press START/PAUSE to begin cooking.
9. When the Zone 1 timer reads 15 minutes, press START/PAUSE. Remove the basket, and use silicone-tipped tongs or a spatula to flip the sandwiches. Reinsert the basket and press START/PAUSE to resume cooking.
10. When both timers read 10 minutes, press START/PAUSE. Remove the Zone 1 basket and transfer the sandwiches to a plate. Place the remaining 2 sandwiches into the basket and insert the basket in the unit. Remove the Zone 2 basket and transfer the zucchini chips to a serving plate. Place the remaining zucchini chips in the basket. Reinsert the basket and press START/PAUSE to resume cooking.
11. When the Zone 1 timer reads 5 minutes, press START/PAUSE. Remove the basket and flip the sandwiches. Reinsert the basket and press START/PAUSE to resume cooking.
12. When cooking is complete, the panini should be

toasted and the zucchini chips golden brown and crisp.
13. Cut each panini in half. Serve hot with zucchini chips on the side.

Nutrition Info:

- (Per serving) Calories: 751; Total fat: 39g; Saturated fat: 9.5g; Carbohydrates: 77g; Fiber: 3.5g; Protein: 23g; Sodium: 1,086mg

Potato And Parsnip Latkes With Baked Apples

Servings:4 | Cooking Time: 20 Minutes

Ingredients:

- FOR THE LATKES
- 2 medium russet potatoes, peeled
- 1 large egg white
- 2 tablespoons all-purpose flour
- ¼ teaspoon garlic powder
- ¼ teaspoon kosher salt
- ¼ teaspoon freshly ground black pepper
- 1 medium parsnip, peeled and shredded
- 2 scallions, thinly sliced
- 2 tablespoons vegetable oil
- FOR THE BAKED APPLES
- 2 Golden Delicious apples, peeled and diced
- 2 tablespoons granulated sugar
- 2 teaspoons unsalted butter, cut into small pieces

Directions:

1. To prep the latkes: Grate the potatoes using the large holes of a box grater. Squeeze as much liquid out of the potatoes as you can into a large bowl. Set the potatoes aside in a separate bowl.
2. Let the potato liquid sit for 5 minutes, during which time the potato starch will settle to the bottom of the bowl. Pour off the water that has risen to the top, leaving the potato starch in the bowl.
3. Add the egg white, flour, salt, and black pepper to the potato starch to form a thick paste. Add the potatoes, parsnip, and scallions and mix well. Divide the mixture into 4 patties. Brush both sides of each patty with the oil.
4. To prep the baked apples: Place the apples in the Zone 2 basket. Sprinkle the sugar and butter over the top.
5. To cook the latkes and apples: Install a crisper plate in the Zone 1 basket. Place the latkes in the basket in a single layer, then insert the basket in the unit. Insert the Zone 2 basket in the unit.
6. Select Zone 1, select AIR FRY, set the temperature to 375°F, and set the timer to 15 minutes.
7. Select Zone 2, select BAKE, set the temperature to 330°F, and set the timer to 20 minutes. Select SMART FINISH.
8. Press START/PAUSE to begin cooking.
9. When both timers read 5 minutes, press START/PAUSE. Remove the Zone 1 basket and use silicone-tipped tongs or a spatula to flip the latkes. Reinsert the basket in the unit. Remove the Zone 2 basket and gently mash the apples with a fork or the back of a spoon. Reinsert the basket and press START/PAUSE to resume cooking.
10. When cooking is complete, the latkes should be golden brown and cooked through and the apples very soft.
11. Transfer the latkes to a plate and serve with apples on the side.

Nutrition Info:

- (Per serving) Calories: 257; Total fat: 9g; Saturated fat: 2g; Carbohydrates: 42g; Fiber: 5.5g; Protein: 4g; Sodium: 91mg

Garlic-herb Fried Squash

Servings: 4 | Cooking Time: 15 Minutes

Ingredients:

- 5 cups halved small pattypan squash (about 1¼ pounds)
- 1 tablespoon olive oil
- 2 garlic cloves, minced
- ½ teaspoon salt
- ¼ teaspoon dried oregano
- ¼ teaspoon dried thyme
- ¼ teaspoon pepper
- 1 tablespoon minced fresh parsley, for serving

Directions:

1. Place the squash in a large bowl.
2. Mix the oil, garlic, salt, oregano, thyme, and pepper; drizzle over the squash. Toss to coat.
3. Place a crisper plate in both drawers. Put the squash in a single layer in each drawer. Insert the drawers into the unit.
4. Select zone 1, then AIR FRY, then set the temperature to 360 degrees F/ 180 degrees C with a 6-minute timer. To match zone 2 settings to zone 1, choose MATCH. To begin, select START/STOP.
5. Remove the squash from the drawers after the timer has finished. Sprinkle with the parsley.

Nutrition Info:

- (Per serving) Calories 58 | Fat 3g | Sodium 296mg | Carbs 6g | Fiber 2g | Sugar 3g | Protein 2g

Beets With Orange Gremolata And Goat's Cheese

Servings: 12 | Cooking Time: 45 Minutes

Ingredients:

- 3 medium fresh golden beets (about 1 pound)
- 3 medium fresh beets (about 1 pound)
- 2 tablespoons lime juice
- 2 tablespoons orange juice
- ½ teaspoon fine sea salt
- 1 tablespoon minced fresh parsley
- 1 tablespoon minced fresh sage
- 1 garlic clove, minced
- 1 teaspoon grated orange zest
- 3 tablespoons crumbled goat's cheese
- 2 tablespoons sunflower kernels

Directions:

1. Scrub the beets and trim the tops by 1 inch.
2. Place the beets on a double thickness of heavy-duty foil (about 24 x 12 inches). Fold the foil around the beets, sealing tightly.
3. Place a crisper plate in both drawers. Put the beets in a single layer in each drawer. Insert the drawers into the unit.
4. Select zone 1, then AIR FRY, then set the temperature to 360 degrees F/ 180 degrees C with a 45-minute timer. To match zone 2 settings to zone 1, choose MATCH. To begin, select START/STOP.
5. Remove the beets from the drawers after the timer has finished. Peel, halve, and slice them when they're cool enough to handle. Place them in a serving bowl.
6. Toss in the lime juice, orange juice, and salt to coat. Sprinkle the beets with the parsley, sage, garlic, and orange zest. The sunflower kernels and goat's cheese go on top.

Nutrition Info:

- (Per serving) Calories 481 | Fat 20g | Sodium 1162mg | Carbs 56g | Fiber 4g | Sugar 9g | Protein 19g

Herb And Lemon Cauliflower

Servings: 4 | Cooking Time: 10 Minutes

Ingredients:

- 1 cauliflower head, cut into florets
- 4 tablespoons olive oil
- ¼ cup fresh parsley
- 1 tablespoon fresh rosemary
- 1 tablespoon fresh thyme
- 1 teaspoon lemon zest, grated
- 2 tablespoons lemon juice
- ½ teaspoon salt
- ¼ teaspoon crushed red pepper flakes

Directions:

1. Toss cauliflower with oil, herbs and the rest of the ingredients in a bowl.
2. Divide the seasoned cauliflower in the air fryer baskets.
3. Return the air fryer basket 1 to Zone 1, and basket 2 to Zone 2 of the Ninja Foodi 2-Basket Air Fryer.
4. Choose the "Air Fry" mode for Zone 1 at 350 degrees F and 10 minutes of cooking time.
5. Select the "MATCH COOK" option to copy the settings for Zone 2.
6. Initiate cooking by pressing the START/PAUSE BUTTON.
7. Serve warm.

Nutrition Info:

- (Per serving) Calories 212 | Fat 11.8g |Sodium 321mg | Carbs 24.6g | Fiber 4.4g | Sugar 8g | Protein 7.3g

Saucy Carrots

Servings: 6 | Cooking Time: 25 Minutes.

Ingredients:

- 1 lb. cup carrots, cut into chunks
- 1 tablespoon sesame oil
- ½ tablespoon ginger, minced
- ½ tablespoon soy sauce
- ½ teaspoon garlic, minced
- ½ tablespoon scallions, chopped, for garnish
- ½ teaspoon sesame seeds for garnish

Directions:

1. Toss all the ginger carrots ingredients, except the sesame seeds and scallions, in a suitable bowl.
2. Divide the carrots in the two crisper plates in a single layer.
3. Return the crisper plates to the Ninja Foodi Dual Zone Air Fryer.
4. Choose the Air Fry mode for Zone 1 and set the temperature to 390 degrees F and the time to 25 minutes.
5. Select the "MATCH" button to copy the settings for Zone 2.
6. Initiate cooking by pressing the START/STOP button.
7. Toss the carrots once cooked halfway through.
8. Garnish with sesame seeds and scallions.
9. Serve warm.

Nutrition Info:

- (Per serving) Calories 206 | Fat 3.4g |Sodium 174mg | Carbs 35g | Fiber 9.4g | Sugar 5.9g | Protein 10.6g

Kale And Spinach Chips

Servings:2 | Cooking Time:6

Ingredients:

- 2 cups spinach, torn in pieces and stem removed
- 2 cups kale, torn in pieces, stems removed
- 1 tablespoon of olive oil
- Sea salt, to taste
- 1/3 cup Parmesan cheese

Directions:

1. Take a bowl and add spinach to it.
2. Take another bowl and add kale to it.
3. Now, season both of them with olive oil, and sea salt.
4. Add kale to zone 1 basket and spinach to zone 2 basket.
5. Select the zone 1 air fry mode at 350 degrees F for 6 minutes.
6. Set zone 2 to AIR FRY mode at 350 for 5 minutes.
7. Once done, take out the crispy chips and sprinkle Parmesan cheese on top.
8. Serve and Enjoy.

Nutrition Info:

- (Per serving) Calories 166| Fat 11.1g| Sodium 355mg | Carbs 8.1g | Fiber1.7 g | Sugar 0.1g | Protein 8.2g

Garlic-rosemary Brussels Sprouts

Servings: 4 | Cooking Time: 8 Minutes

Ingredients:

- 3 tablespoons olive oil
- 2 garlic cloves, minced
- ½ teaspoon salt
- ¼ teaspoon black pepper
- 455g Brussels sprouts, halved
- ½ cup panko bread crumbs
- 1-½ teaspoons rosemary, minced

Directions:

1. Toss the Brussels sprouts with crumbs and the rest of the ingredients in a bowl.
2. Divide the sprouts into the Ninja Foodi 2 Baskets Air Fryer baskets.
3. Return the air fryer basket 1 to Zone 1, and basket 2 to Zone 2 of the Ninja Foodi 2-Basket Air Fryer.
4. Choose the "Air Fry" mode for Zone 1 at 350 degrees F and 8 minutes of cooking time.
5. Select the "MATCH COOK" option to copy the settings for Zone 2.
6. Initiate cooking by pressing the START/PAUSE BUTTON.
7. Toss the Brussels sprouts once cooked halfway through.
8. Serve warm.

Nutrition Info:

- (Per serving) Calories 231 | Fat 9g |Sodium 271mg | Carbs 32.8g | Fiber 6.4g | Sugar 7g | Protein 6.3g

Buffalo Bites

Servings: 6 | Cooking Time: 30 Minutes

Ingredients:

- For the bites:
- 1 small cauliflower head, cut into florets
- 2 tablespoons olive oil
- 3 tablespoons buffalo wing sauce
- 3 tablespoons butter, melted
- For the dip:
- 1½ cups 2% cottage cheese
- ¼ cup fat-free plain Greek yogurt
- ¼ cup crumbled blue cheese
- 1 sachet ranch salad dressing mix
- Celery sticks (optional)

Directions:

1. In a large bowl, combine the cauliflower and oil; toss to coat.
2. Place a crisper plate in each drawer. Put the coated cauliflower florets in each drawer in a single layer. Place the drawers in the unit.
3. Select zone 1, then AIR FRY, then set the temperature to 360 degrees F/ 180 degrees C with a 15-minute timer. To match zone 2 settings to zone 1, choose MATCH. To begin, select START/STOP.
4. Remove the cauliflower from the drawers after the timer has finished.
5. Combine the buffalo sauce and melted butter in a large mixing bowl. Put in the cauliflower and toss to coat. Place on a serving dish and serve.
6. Combine the dip ingredients in a small bowl. Serve with the cauliflower and celery sticks, if desired.

Nutrition Info:

- (Per serving) Calories 203 | Fat 13g | Sodium 1470mg | Carbs 13g | Fiber 4g | Sugar 1g | Protein 9g

Stuffed Tomatoes

Servings:2 | Cooking Time:8

Ingredients:

- 2 cups brown rice, cooked
- 1 cup of tofu, grilled and chopped
- 4 large red tomatoes
- 4 tablespoons basil, chopped
- 1/4 tablespoon olive oil
- Salt and black pepper, to taste
- 2 tablespoons of lemon juice
- 1 teaspoon of red chili powder
- ½ cup Parmesan cheese

Directions:

1. Take a large bowl and mix rice, tofu, basil, olive oil, salt, black pepper, lemon juice, and chili powder.
2. Take four large tomatoes and center core them.
3. Fill the cavity with the rice mixture.
4. Top it off with the cheese sprinkle.
5. Divide the tomatoes into two air fryer baskets.
6. turn on zone one basket and cook tomatoes at AIR-FRY mode, for 8 minutes at 400 degrees F.
7. Select the MATCH button for zone two baskets, which cooks food by copying the setting across both zones.
8. Serve and enjoy.

Nutrition Info:

- (Per serving) Calories 1034| Fat 24.2g| Sodium 527mg | Carbs165 g | Fiber12.1 g | Sugar 1.2g | Protein 43.9g

Satay-style Tempeh With Corn Fritters

Servings:4 | Cooking Time: 15 Minutes

Ingredients:

- FOR THE TEMPEH
- 1 (8-ounce) package tempeh
- 3 tablespoons fresh lemon juice, divided
- 2 tablespoons soy sauce, divided
- 2 garlic cloves, chopped
- ½ teaspoon ground turmeric
- 2 tablespoons vegetable oil
- ¾ cup canned full-fat coconut milk
- 4 tablespoons peanut butter
- 1 teaspoon light brown sugar
- ½ teaspoon red pepper flakes
- 1 scallion, chopped
- FOR THE CORN FRITTERS
- 2 cups frozen corn, thawed and drained
- 2 scallions, thinly sliced
- ¼ cup chopped fresh cilantro
- ¼ teaspoon kosher salt
- 2 large eggs
- ½ cup all-purpose flour
- 2 tablespoons vegetable oil

Directions:

1. To prep the tempeh: Slice the tempeh into ¼-inch-thick slabs.
2. In a large bowl, combine 2 tablespoons of lemon juice, 1 tablespoon of soy sauce, the garlic, turmeric, and oil.
3. Add the tempeh to the marinade and toss to coat the pieces. Let marinate for 15 minutes.
4. In a medium bowl, whisk together the coconut milk, peanut butter, remaining 1 tablespoon of lemon juice, remaining 1 tablespoon of soy sauce, brown sugar, red pepper flakes, and scallion. Set aside.
5. To prep the corn fritters: In a large bowl, combine the corn, scallions, cilantro, and salt. Mix in the eggs and flour until everything is well combined.
6. To cook the tempeh and fritters: Install a broil rack in the Zone 1 basket. Arrange the tempeh in a single layer on the rack and insert the basket in the unit. Install a crisper plate in the Zone 2 basket. Spoon 2 tablespoons of corn fritter batter into each corner of the basket and drizzle with oil. Flatten slightly with the back of the spoon and insert the basket in the unit.
7. Select Zone 1, select AIR BROIL, set the temperature to 400°F, and set the timer to 8 minutes.
8. Select Zone 2, select AIR FRY, set the temperature to 375°F, and set the timer to 15 minutes. Select SMART FINISH.
9. Press START/PAUSE to begin cooking.
10. When the Zone 2 timer reads 5 minutes, press START/PAUSE. Remove the basket and use silicone-tipped tongs or a spatula to flip the corn fritters. Reinsert the basket and press START/PAUSE to resume cooking.
11. When cooking is complete, the tempeh will be golden brown and the corn fritters set in the center and browned on the edges.
12. Serve the tempeh with the peanut sauce for dipping and the corn fritters on the side.

Nutrition Info:

- (Per serving) Calories: 578; Total fat: 40g; Saturated fat: 14g; Carbohydrates: 39g; Fiber: 3.5g; Protein: 24g; Sodium: 815mg

Balsamic-glazed Tofu With Roasted Butternut Squash

Servings:4 | Cooking Time: 40 Minutes

Ingredients:

- FOR THE BALSAMIC TOFU
- 2 tablespoons balsamic vinegar
- 1 tablespoon maple syrup
- 1 teaspoon soy sauce
- 1 teaspoon Dijon mustard
- 1 (14-ounce) package firm tofu, drained and cut into large cubes
- 1 tablespoon canola oil
- FOR THE BUTTERNUT SQUASH
- 1 small butternut squash
- 1 tablespoon canola oil
- 1 teaspoon light brown sugar
- ¼ teaspoon kosher salt
- ¼ teaspoon freshly ground black pepper

Directions:

1. To prep the balsamic tofu: In a large bowl, whisk to-

gether the vinegar, maple syrup, soy sauce, and mustard. Add the tofu and stir to coat. Cover and marinate for at least 20 minutes (or up to overnight in the refrigerator).
2. To prep the butternut squash: Peel the squash and cut in half lengthwise. Remove and discard the seeds. Cut the squash crosswise into ½-inch-thick slices.
3. Brush the squash pieces with the oil, then sprinkle with the brown sugar, salt, and black pepper.
4. To cook the tofu and squash: Install a crisper plate in each of the two baskets. Place the tofu in the Zone 1 basket, drizzle with the oil, and insert the basket in the unit. Place the squash in the Zone 2 basket and insert the basket in the unit.
5. Select Zone 1, select AIR FRY, set the temperature to 400°F, and set the timer to 10 minutes.
6. Select Zone 2, select ROAST, set the temperature to 400°F, and set the timer to 40 minutes. Select SMART FINISH.
7. Press START/PAUSE to begin cooking.
8. When cooking is complete, the tofu will have begun to crisp and brown around the edges and the squash should be tender. Serve hot.

Nutrition Info:

- (Per serving) Calories: 253; Total fat: 11g; Saturated fat: 1g; Carbohydrates: 30g; Fiber: 4.5g; Protein: 11g; Sodium: 237mg

Fried Patty Pan Squash

Servings: 6 | Cooking Time: 15 Minutes

Ingredients:

- 5 cups small pattypan squash, halved
- 1 tablespoon olive oil
- 2 garlic cloves, minced
- ½ teaspoon salt
- ¼ teaspoon dried oregano
- ¼ teaspoon dried thyme
- ¼ teaspoon pepper
- 1 tablespoon minced parsley

Directions:

1. Rub the squash with oil, garlic and the rest of the ingredients.
2. Spread the squash in the air fryer baskets.
3. Return the air fryer basket 1 to Zone 1, and basket 2 to Zone 2 of the Ninja Foodi 2-Basket Air Fryer.
4. Choose the "Air Fry" mode for Zone 1 at 375 degrees F and 15 minutes of cooking time.
5. Select the "MATCH COOK" option to copy the settings for Zone 2.
6. Initiate cooking by pressing the START/PAUSE BUTTON.
7. Flip the squash once cooked halfway through.
8. Garnish with parsley.
9. Serve warm.

Nutrition Info:

- (Per serving) Calories 208 | Fat 5g |Sodium 1205mg | Carbs 34.1g | Fiber 7.8g | Sugar 2.5g | Protein 5.9g

Brussels Sprouts

Servings:2 | Cooking Time:20

Ingredients:

- 2 pounds Brussels sprouts
- 2 tablespoons avocado oil
- Salt and pepper, to taste
- 1 cup pine nuts, roasted

Directions:

1. Trim the bottom of Brussels sprouts.
2. Take a bowl and combine the avocado oil, salt, and black pepper.
3. Toss the Brussels sprouts well.
4. Divide it in both air fryer baskets.
5. For the zone 1 basket use AIR fry mode for 20 minutes at 390 degrees F.
6. Select the MATCH button for the zone 2 basket.
7. Once the Brussels sprouts get crisp and tender, take out and serve.

Nutrition Info:

- (Per serving) Calories 672| Fat 50g| Sodium 115mg | Carbs 51g | Fiber 20.2g | Sugar 12.3g | Protein 25g

Desserts Recipes

Cinnamon Sugar Dessert Fries

Servings: 4 | Cooking Time: 15 Minutes

Ingredients:

- 2 sweet potatoes
- 1 tablespoon butter, melted
- 1 teaspoon butter, melted
- 2 tablespoons sugar
- ½ teaspoon ground cinnamon

Directions:

1. Peel and cut the sweet potatoes into skinny fries.
2. Coat the fries with 1 tablespoon of butter.
3. Install a crisper plate into each drawer. Place half the sweet potatoes in the zone 1 drawer and half in zone 2's, then insert the drawers into the unit.
4. Select zone 1, select AIR FRY, set temperature to 390 degrees F/ 200 degrees C, and set time to 15 minutes. Select MATCH to match zone 2 settings to zone 1. Press the START/STOP button to begin cooking.
5. When the time reaches 11 minutes, press START/STOP to pause the unit. Remove the drawers and flip the fries. Re-insert the drawers into the unit and press START/STOP to resume cooking.
6. Meanwhile, mix the 1 teaspoon of butter, the sugar, and the cinnamon in a large bowl.
7. When the fries are done, add them to the bowl, and toss them to coat.
8. Serve and enjoy!

Nutrition Info:

- (Per serving) Calories 110 | Fat 4g | Sodium 51mg | Carbs 18g | Fiber 2g | Sugar 10g | Protein 1g

Apple Crisp

Servings: 8 | Cooking Time: 14 Minutes.

Ingredients:

- 3 cups apples, chopped
- 1 tablespoon pure maple syrup
- 2 teaspoons lemon juice
- 3 tablespoons all-purpose flour
- ⅓ cup quick oats
- ¼ cup brown sugar
- 2 tablespoons light butter, melted
- ½ teaspoon cinnamon

Directions:

1. Toss the chopped apples with 1 tablespoon of all-purpose flour, cinnamon, maple syrup, and lemon juice in a suitable bowl.
2. Divide the apples in the two air fryer baskets with their crisper plates.
3. Whisk oats, brown sugar, and remaining all-purpose flour in a small bowl.
4. Stir in melted butter, then divide this mixture over the apples.
5. Return the crisper plate to the Ninja Foodi Dual Zone Air Fryer.
6. Select the Bake mode for Zone 1 and set the temperature to 375 degrees F and the time to 14 minutes.
7. Select the "MATCH" button to copy the settings for Zone 2.
8. Initiate cooking by pressing the START/STOP button.
9. Enjoy fresh.

Nutrition Info:

- (Per serving) Calories 258 | Fat 12.4g |Sodium 79mg | Carbs 34.3g | Fiber 1g | Sugar 17g | Protein 3.2g

Honey Lime Pineapple

Servings: 4 | Cooking Time: 10 Minutes

Ingredients:

- 562g pineapple chunks
- 55g brown sugar
- 30ml lime juice
- 63g honey

Directions:

1. In a bowl, mix pineapple, honey, lime juice, and brown sugar. Cover and place in refrigerator for 1 hour.
2. Insert a crisper plate in Ninja Foodi air fryer baskets.
3. Remove pineapple chunks from the marinade and place in both baskets.
4. Select zone 1 then select "air fry" mode and set the temperature to 390 degrees F for 10 minutes. Press "match" to match zone 2 settings to zone 1. Press "start/stop" to begin. Stir halfway through.

Nutrition Info:

- (Per serving) Calories 153 | Fat 0.2g |Sodium 5mg | Carbs 40.5g | Fiber 2g | Sugar 35.7g | Protein 0.8g

Chocolate Chip Cake

Servings:4 | Cooking Time:15

Ingredients:

- Salt, pinch
- 2 eggs, whisked
- ½ cup brown sugar
- ½ cup butter, melted
- 10 tablespoons of almond milk
- ¼ teaspoon of vanilla extract
- ½ teaspoon of baking powder
- 1 cup all-purpose flour
- 1 cup of chocolate chips
- ½ cup of cocoa powder

Directions:

1. Take 2 round baking pan that fits inside the baskets of the air fryer.
2. layer it with baking paper, cut it to the size of a baking pan.
3. In a bowl, whisk the egg, brown sugar, butter, almond milk, and vanilla extract.
4. Whisk it all very well with an electric hand beater.
5. In a second bowl, mix the flour, cocoa powder, baking powder, and salt.
6. Now, mix the dry ingredients slowly with the wet ingredients.
7. Now, at the end fold in the chocolate chips.
8. Incorporate all the ingredients well.
9. Divide this batter into the round baking pan.
10. Set the time for zone 1 to 16 minutes at 350 degrees F at AIR FRY mode.
11. Select the MATCH button for the zone 2 baskets.
12. Check if not done, and let it AIR FRY for one more minute.
13. Once it is done, serve.

Nutrition Info:

- (Per serving) Calories 736| Fat45.5g| Sodium 356mg | Carbs 78.2g | Fiber 6.1g | Sugar 32.7g | Protein11.5 g

Chocolate Cookies

Servings: 18 | Cooking Time: 7 Minutes

Ingredients:

- 96g flour
- 57g butter, softened
- 15ml milk
- 7.5g cocoa powder
- 80g chocolate chips
- ½ tsp vanilla
- 35g sugar
- ¼ tsp baking soda
- Pinch of salt

Directions:

1. In a bowl, mix flour, cocoa powder, sugar, baking soda, vanilla, butter, milk, and salt until well combined.
2. Add chocolate chips and mix well.
3. Insert a crisper plate in Ninja Foodi air fryer baskets.
4. Make cookies from the mixture and place in both baskets.
5. Select zone 1 then select "air fry" mode and set the temperature to 360 degrees F for 7 minutes. Press "match" to match zone 2 settings to zone 1. Press "start/stop" to begin.

Nutrition Info:

- (Per serving) Calories 82 | Fat 4.1g |Sodium 47mg | Carbs 10.7g | Fiber 0.4g | Sugar 6.2g | Protein 1g

Apple Crumble Peach Crumble

Servings:8 | Cooking Time: 20 Minutes

Ingredients:

- FOR THE APPLE CRUMBLE
- ½ cup packed light brown sugar
- ¼ cup all-purpose flour
- ¼ cup rolled oats
- 2 tablespoons unsalted butter, at room temperature
- ½ teaspoon ground cinnamon
- ¼ teaspoon ground nutmeg
- ⅛ teaspoon kosher salt
- 4 medium Granny Smith apples, sliced
- FOR THE PEACH CRUMBLE
- ½ cup packed light brown sugar
- ¼ cup all-purpose flour
- ¼ cup rolled oats
- 2 tablespoons unsalted butter, at room temperature
- ½ teaspoon ground cinnamon
- ⅛ teaspoon kosher salt
- 4 peaches, peeled and sliced

Directions:

1. To prep the apple crumble: In a medium bowl, combine the brown sugar, flour, oats, butter, cinnamon, nutmeg, and salt and mix well. The mixture will be dry and crumbly.
2. To prep the peach crumble: In a medium bowl, combine the brown sugar, flour, oats, butter, cinnamon, and salt and mix well. The mixture will be dry and crumbly.
3. To cook both crumbles: Spread the apples in the Zone 1 basket in an even layer. Top evenly with the apple crumble topping and insert the basket in the unit. Spread the peaches in the Zone 2 basket in an even layer. Top with the peach crumble topping and insert the basket in the unit.
4. Select Zone 1, select BAKE, set the temperature to 350°F, and set the timer to 20 minutes. Select MATCH COOK to match Zone 2 settings to Zone 1.
5. Press START/PAUSE to begin cooking.

6. When cooking is complete, the fruit will be tender and the crumble topping crisp and golden brown. Serve warm or at room temperature.

Nutrition Info:

- (Per serving) Calories: 300; Total fat: 6.5g; Saturated fat: 3.5g; Carbohydrates: 59g; Fiber: 5.5g; Protein: 2g; Sodium: 45mg

Jelly Donuts

Servings: 4 | Cooking Time: 5 Minutes

Ingredients:

- 1 package Pillsbury Grands (Homestyle)
- ½ cup seedless raspberry jelly
- 1 tablespoon butter, melted
- ½ cup sugar

Directions:

1. Install a crisper plate in both drawers. Place half of the biscuits in the zone 1 drawer and half in zone 2's, then insert the drawers into the unit. You may need to cook in batches.
2. Select zone 1, select AIR FRY, set temperature to 390 degrees F/ 200 degrees C, and set time to 22 minutes. Select MATCH to match zone 2 settings to zone 1. Press the START/STOP button to begin cooking.
3. Place the sugar into a wide bowl with a flat bottom.
4. Baste all sides of the cooked biscuits with the melted butter and roll in the sugar to cover completely.
5. Using a long cake tip, pipe 1–2 tablespoons of raspberry jelly into each biscuit. You've now got raspberry-filled donuts!

Nutrition Info:

- (Per serving) Calories 252 | Fat 7g | Sodium 503mg | Carbs 45g | Fiber 0g | Sugar 23g | Protein 3g

Bread Pudding

Servings: 4 | Cooking Time: 15 Minutes

Ingredients:

- 2 cups bread cubes
- 1 egg
- ⅔ cup heavy cream
- ½ teaspoon vanilla extract
- ¼ cup sugar
- ¼ cup chocolate chips

Directions:

1. Grease two 4 inches baking dish with a cooking spray.
2. Divide the bread cubes in the baking dishes and sprinkle chocolate chips on top.
3. Beat egg with cream, sugar and vanilla in a bowl.
4. Divide this mixture in the baking dishes.
5. Place one pan in each air fryer basket.
6. Return the air fryer basket 1 to Zone 1, and basket 2 to Zone 2 of the Ninja Foodi 2-Basket Air Fryer.
7. Choose the "Air Fry" mode for Zone 1 at 350 degrees F and 15 minutes of cooking time.
8. Select the "MATCH COOK" option to copy the settings for Zone 2.
9. Initiate cooking by pressing the START/PAUSE BUTTON.
10. Allow the pudding to cool and serve.

Nutrition Info:

- (Per serving) Calories 149 | Fat 1.2g |Sodium 3mg | Carbs 37.6g | Fiber 5.8g | Sugar 29g | Protein 1.1g

Biscuit Doughnuts

Servings: 8 | Cooking Time: 15 Minutes.

Ingredients:

- ½ cup white sugar
- 1 teaspoon cinnamon
- ½ cup powdered sugar
- 1 can pre-made biscuit dough
- Coconut oil
- Melted butter to brush biscuits

Directions:

1. Place all the biscuits on a cutting board and cut holes in the center of each biscuit using a cookie cutter.
2. Grease the crisper plate with coconut oil.
3. Place the biscuits in the two crisper plates while keeping them 1 inch apart.
4. Return the crisper plates to the Ninja Foodi Dual Zone Air Fryer.
5. Choose the Air Fry mode for Zone 1 and set the temperature to 375 degrees F and the time to 15 minutes.
6. Select the "MATCH" button to copy the settings for Zone 2.
7. Initiate cooking by pressing the START/STOP button.
8. Brush all the donuts with melted butter and sprinkle cinnamon and sugar on top.
9. Air fry these donuts for one minute more.
10. Enjoy!

Nutrition Info:

- (Per serving) Calories 192 | Fat 9.3g |Sodium 133mg | Carbs 27.1g | Fiber 1.4g | Sugar 19g | Protein 3.2g

Healthy Semolina Pudding

Servings: 4 | Cooking Time: 20 Minutes

Ingredients:

- 45g semolina
- 1 tsp vanilla
- 500ml milk
- 115g caster sugar

Directions:

1. Mix semolina and ½ cup milk in a bowl. Slowly add the remaining milk, sugar, and vanilla and mix well.
2. Pour the mixture into four greased ramekins.
3. Insert a crisper plate in the Ninja Foodi air fryer baskets.
4. Place ramekins in both baskets.
5. Select zone 1, then select "air fry" mode and set the temperature to 300 degrees F for 20 minutes. Press "match" to match zone 2 settings to zone 1. Press "start/stop" to begin.

Nutrition Info:

- (Per serving) Calories 209 | Fat 2.7g |Sodium 58mg | Carbs 41.5g | Fiber 0.6g | Sugar 30.6g | Protein 5.8g

Cinnamon-sugar "churros" With Caramel Sauce

Servings:4 | Cooking Time: 10 Minutes

Ingredients:

- FOR THE "CHURROS"
- 1 sheet frozen puff pastry, thawed
- Butter-flavored cooking spray
- 1 tablespoon granulated sugar
- 1 teaspoon ground cinnamon
- FOR THE CARAMEL SAUCE
- ½ cup packed light brown sugar
- 2 tablespoons unsalted butter, cut into small pieces
- ¼ cup heavy (whipping) cream
- 2 teaspoons vanilla extract
- ⅛ teaspoon kosher salt

Directions:

1. To prep the "churros": Cut the puff pastry crosswise into 4 rectangles. Fold each piece in half lengthwise to make a long thin "churro."
2. To prep the caramel sauce: Measure the brown sugar, butter, cream, and vanilla into an ovenproof ramekin or bowl (no need to stir).
3. To cook the "churros" and caramel sauce: Install a crisper plate in the Zone 1 basket. Place the "churros" in the basket and insert the basket in the unit. Place the ramekin in the Zone 2 basket and insert the basket in the unit.
4. Select Zone 1, select AIR FRY, set the temperature to 330°F, and set the timer to 10 minutes.
5. Select Zone 2, select BAKE, set the temperature to 350°F, and set the timer to 10 minutes. Select SMART FINISH.
6. Press START/PAUSE to begin cooking.
7. When the Zone 2 timer reads 5 minutes, press START/PAUSE. Remove the basket and stir the caramel. Reinsert the basket and press START/PAUSE to resume cooking.
8. When cooking is complete, the "churros" will be golden brown and cooked through and the caramel sauce smooth.
9. Spritz each "churro" with cooking spray and sprinkle generously with the granulated sugar and cinnamon.
10. Stir the salt into the caramel sauce. Let cool for 5 to 10 minutes before serving. Note that the caramel will thicken as it cools.

Nutrition Info:

- (Per serving) Calories: 460; Total fat: 26g; Saturated fat: 14g; Carbohydrates: 60g; Fiber: 1.5g; Protein: 5g; Sodium: 254mg

Lemon Sugar Cookie Bars Monster Sugar Cookie Bars

Servings:12 | Cooking Time: 18 Minutes

Ingredients:

- FOR THE LEMON COOKIE BARS
- Grated zest and juice of 1 lemon
- ½ cup granulated sugar
- 4 tablespoons (½ stick) unsalted butter, at room temperature
- 1 large egg yolk
- 1 teaspoon vanilla extract
- ⅛ teaspoon baking powder
- ½ cup plus 2 tablespoons all-purpose flour
- FOR THE MONSTER COOKIE BARS
- ½ cup granulated sugar
- 4 tablespoons (½ stick) unsalted butter, at room temperature
- 1 large egg yolk
- 1 teaspoon vanilla extract
- ⅛ teaspoon baking powder
- ½ cup plus 2 tablespoons all-purpose flour
- ¼ cup rolled oats
- ¼ cup M&M's
- ¼ cup peanut butter chips

Directions:

1. To prep the lemon cookie bars: In a large bowl, rub together the lemon zest and sugar. Add the butter and use a hand mixer to beat until light and fluffy.
2. Beat in the egg yolk, vanilla, and lemon juice. Mix in

the baking powder and flour.
3. To prep the monster cookie bars: In a large bowl, with a hand mixer, beat the sugar and butter until light and fluffy.
4. Beat in the egg yolk and vanilla. Mix in the baking powder and flour. Stir in the oats, M&M's, and peanut butter chips.
5. To cook the cookie bars: Line both baskets with aluminum foil. Press the lemon cookie dough into the Zone 1 basket and insert the basket in the unit. Press the monster cookie dough into the Zone 2 basket and insert the basket in the unit.
6. Select Zone 1, select BAKE, set the temperature to 330°F, and set the timer to 18 minutes. Press MATCH COOK to match Zone 2 settings to Zone 1.
7. Press START/PAUSE to begin cooking.
8. When cooking is complete, the cookies should be set in the middle and have begun to pull away from the sides of the basket.
9. Let the cookies cool completely, about 1 hour. Cut each basket into 6 bars for a total of 12 bars.

Nutrition Info:

• (Per serving) Calories: 191; Total fat: 8.5g; Saturated fat: 5g; Carbohydrates: 27g; Fiber: 0.5g; Protein: 2g; Sodium: 3mg

Zesty Cranberry Scones

Servings: 8 | Cooking Time: 16 Minutes.

Ingredients:

- 4 cups of flour
- ½ cup brown sugar
- 2 tablespoons baking powder
- ½ teaspoon ground nutmeg
- ½ teaspoon salt
- ½ cup butter, chilled and diced
- 2 cups fresh cranberry
- ⅔ cup sugar
- 2 tablespoons orange zest
- 1 ¼ cups half and half cream
- 2 eggs

Directions:

1. Whisk flour with baking powder, salt, nutmeg, and both the sugars in a bowl.
2. Stir in egg and cream, mix well to form a smooth dough.
3. Fold in cranberries along with the orange zest.
4. Knead this dough well on a work surface.
5. Cut 3-inch circles out of the dough.
6. Divide the scones in the crisper plates and spray them with cooking oil.
7. Return the crisper plates to the Ninja Foodi Dual Zone Air Fryer.
8. Choose the Air Fry mode for Zone 1 and set the temperature to 375 degrees F and the time to 16 minutes.
9. Select the "MATCH" button to copy the settings for Zone 2.
10. Initiate cooking by pressing the START/STOP button.
11. Flip the scones once cooked halfway and resume cooking.
12. Enjoy!

Nutrition Info:

• (Per serving) Calories 204 | Fat 9g |Sodium 91mg | Carbs 27g | Fiber 2.4g | Sugar 15g | Protein 1.3g

Walnuts Fritters

Servings: 6 | Cooking Time: 15 Minutes.

Ingredients:

- 1 cup all-purpose flour
- ½ cup walnuts, chopped
- ¼ cup white sugar
- ¼ cup milk
- 1 egg
- 1 ½ teaspoons baking powder
- 1 pinch salt
- Cooking spray
- 2 tablespoons white sugar
- ½ teaspoon ground cinnamon
- Glaze:
- ½ cup confectioners› sugar
- 1 tablespoon milk
- ½ teaspoon caramel extract
- ¼ teaspoons ground cinnamon

Directions:

1. Layer both crisper plate with parchment paper.
2. Grease the parchment paper with cooking spray.
3. Whisk flour with milk, ¼ cup of sugar, egg, baking powder, and salt in a small bowl.
4. Separately mix 2 tablespoons of sugar with cinnamon in another bowl, toss in walnuts and mix well to coat.
5. Stir in flour mixture and mix until combined.
6. Drop the fritters mixture using a cookie scoop into the two crisper plate.
7. Return the crisper plate to the Ninja Foodi Dual Zone Air Fryer.
8. Choose the Air Fry mode for Zone 1 and set the temperature to 375 degrees F and the time to 15 minutes.
9. Select the "MATCH" button to copy the settings for Zone 2.
10. Initiate cooking by pressing the START/STOP button.
11. Flip the fritters once cooked halfway through, then resume cooking.
12. Meanwhile, whisk milk, caramel extract, confection-

ers' sugar, and cinnamon in a bowl.
13. Transfer fritters to a wire rack and allow them to cool.
14. Drizzle with a glaze over the fritters.

Nutrition Info:

• (Per serving) Calories 391 | Fat 24g |Sodium 142mg | Carbs 38.5g | Fiber 3.5g | Sugar 21g | Protein 6.6g

Apple Fritters

Servings: 14 | Cooking Time: 10 Minutes

Ingredients:

- 2 large apples
- 2 cups all-purpose flour
- ½ cup granulated sugar
- 1 tablespoon baking powder
- 1 teaspoon salt
- 1 teaspoon ground cinnamon
- ½ teaspoon ground nutmeg
- ¼ teaspoon ground cloves
- ¾ cup apple cider or apple juice
- 2 eggs
- 3 tablespoons butter, melted
- 1 teaspoon vanilla extract
- For the apple cider glaze:
- 2 cups powdered sugar
- ¼ cup apple cider or apple juice
- ½ teaspoon ground cinnamon
- ¼ teaspoon ground nutmeg

Directions:

1. Peel and core the apples, then cut them into ¼-inch cubes. Spread the apple chunks out on a kitchen towel to absorb any excess moisture.
2. In a mixing bowl, combine the flour, sugar, baking powder, salt, and spices.
3. Add the apple chunks and combine well.
4. Whisk together the apple cider, eggs, melted butter, and vanilla in a small bowl.
5. Combine the wet and dry ingredients in a large mixing bowl.
6. Install a crisper plate in both drawers. Use an ice cream scoop to scoop 3 to 4 dollops of fritter dough into the zone 1 drawer and 3 to 4 dollops into the zone 2 drawer. Insert the drawers into the unit. You may need to cook in batches.
7. Select zone 1, select BAKE, set temperature to 390 degrees F/ 200 degrees C, and set time to 10 minutes. Select MATCH to match zone 2 settings to zone 1. Press the START/STOP button to begin cooking.
8. Meanwhile, make the glaze: Whisk the powdered sugar, apple cider, and spices together until smooth.
9. When the fritters are cooked, drizzle the glaze over them. Let sit for 10 minutes until the glaze sets.

Nutrition Info:

• (Per serving) Calories 221 | Fat 3g | Sodium 288mg | Carbs 46g | Fiber 2g | Sugar 29g | Protein 3g

Oreo Rolls

Servings: 9 | Cooking Time: 8 Minutes.

Ingredients:

- 1 crescent sheet roll
- 9 Oreo cookies
- Cinnamon powder, to serve
- Powdered sugar, to serve

Directions:

1. Spread the crescent sheet roll and cut it into 9 equal squares.
2. Place one cookie at the center of each square.
3. Wrap each square around the cookies and press the ends to seal.
4. Place half of the wrapped cookies in each crisper plate.
5. Return the crisper plates to the Ninja Foodi Dual Zone Air Fryer.
6. Select the Bake mode for Zone 1 and set the temperature to 360 degrees F and the time to 4-6 minutes.
7. Select the "MATCH" button to copy the settings for Zone 2.
8. Initiate cooking by pressing the START/STOP button.
9. Check for the doneness of the cookie rolls if they are golden brown, else cook 1-2 minutes more.
10. Garnish the rolls with sugar and cinnamon.
11. Serve.

Nutrition Info:

• (Per serving) Calories 175 | Fat 13.1g |Sodium 154mg | Carbs 14g | Fiber 0.8g | Sugar 8.9g | Protein 0.7g

Pumpkin Hand Pies Blueberry Hand Pies

Servings:4 | Cooking Time: 15 Minutes

Ingredients:

- FOR THE PUMPKIN HAND PIES
- ½ cup pumpkin pie filling (from a 15-ounce can)
- ⅓ cup half-and-half
- 1 large egg
- ½ refrigerated pie crust (from a 14.1-ounce package)
- 1 large egg yolk
- 1 tablespoon whole milk
- FOR THE BLUEBERRY HAND PIES
- ¼ cup blueberries
- 2 tablespoons granulated sugar
- 1 tablespoon grated lemon zest (optional)
- ¼ teaspoon cornstarch
- 1 teaspoon fresh lemon juice
- ⅛ teaspoon kosher salt
- ½ refrigerated pie crust (from a 14.1-ounce package)
- 1 large egg yolk
- 1 tablespoon whole milk
- ½ teaspoon turbinado sugar

Directions:

1. To prep the pumpkin hand pies: In a small bowl, mix the pumpkin pie filling, half-and-half, and whole egg until well combined and smooth.
2. Cut the dough in half to form two wedges. Divide the pumpkin pie filling between the wedges. Fold the crust over to completely encase the filling. Using a fork, crimp the edges, forming a tight seal.
3. In a small bowl, whisk together the egg yolk and milk. Brush over the pastry. Carefully cut two small vents in the top of each pie.
4. To prep the blueberry hand pies: In a small bowl, combine the blueberries, granulated sugar, lemon zest (if using), cornstarch, lemon juice, and salt.
5. Cut the dough in half to form two wedges. Divide the blueberry filling between the wedges. Fold the crust over to completely encase the filling. Using a fork, crimp the edges, forming a tight seal.
6. In a small bowl, whisk together the egg yolk and milk. Brush over the pastry. Sprinkle with the turbinado sugar. Carefully cut two small vents in the top of each pie.
7. To cook the hand pies: Install a crisper plate in each of the two baskets. Place the pumpkin hand pies in the Zone 1 basket and insert the basket in the unit. Place the blueberry hand pies in the Zone 2 basket and insert the basket in the unit.
8. Select Zone 1, select AIR FRY, set the temperature to 350°F, and set the timer to 15 minutes. Select MATCH COOK to match Zone 2 settings to Zone 1.
9. Press START/PAUSE to begin cooking.
10. When cooking is complete, the pie crust should be crisp and golden brown and the filling bubbling.
11. Let the hand pies cool for at least 30 minutes before serving.

Nutrition Info:

- (Per serving) Calories: 588; Total fat: 33g; Saturated fat: 14g; Carbohydrates: 68g; Fiber: 0.5g; Protein: 10g; Sodium: 583mg

Baked Apples

Servings: 4 | Cooking Time: 15 Minutes

Ingredients:

- 4 apples
- 6 teaspoons raisins
- 2 teaspoons chopped walnuts
- 2 teaspoons honey
- ½ teaspoon cinnamon

Directions:

1. Chop off the head of the apples and scoop out the flesh from the center.
2. Stuff the apples with raisins, walnuts, honey and cinnamon.
3. Place these apples in the air fryer basket 1.
4. Return the air fryer basket 1 to Zone 1 of the Ninja Foodi 2-Basket Air Fryer.
5. Choose the "Air Fry" mode for Zone 1 and set the temperature to 350 degrees F and 15 minutes of cooking time.
6. Initiate cooking by pressing the START/PAUSE BUTTON.
7. Serve.

Nutrition Info:

- (Per serving) Calories 175 | Fat 13.1g |Sodium 154mg | Carbs 14g | Fiber 0.8g | Sugar 8.9g | Protein 0.7g

Lava Cake

Servings: 4 | Cooking Time: 10 Minutes

Ingredients:

- 1 cup semi-sweet chocolate chips
- 8 tablespoons butter
- 4 eggs
- 2 teaspoons vanilla extract
- ½ teaspoon salt
- 6 tablespoons all-purpose flour
- 1 cup powdered sugar
- For the chocolate filling:
- 2 tablespoons Nutella
- 1 tablespoon butter, softened
- 1 tablespoon powdered sugar

Directions:

1. Heat the chocolate chips and butter in a medium-sized microwave-safe bowl in 30-second intervals until thoroughly melted and smooth, stirring after each interval.
2. Whisk together the eggs, vanilla, salt, flour, and powdered sugar in a mixing bowl.
3. Combine the Nutella, softened butter, and powdered sugar in a separate bowl.
4. Spray 4 ramekins with oil and fill them halfway with the chocolate chip mixture. Fill each ramekin halfway with Nutella, then top with the remaining chocolate chip mixture, making sure the Nutella is well covered.
5. Install a crisper plate in both drawers. Place 2 ramekins in each drawer and insert the drawers into the unit.
6. Select zone 1, select AIR FRY, set temperature to 390 degrees F/ 200 degrees C, and set time to 22 minutes. Select MATCH to match zone 2 settings to zone 1. Press the START/STOP button to begin cooking.
7. Serve hot.

Nutrition Info:

• (Per serving) Calories 338 | Fat 21.2g | Sodium 1503mg | Carbs 5.1g | Fiber 0.3g | Sugar 4.6g | Protein 29.3g

Moist Chocolate Espresso Muffins

Servings: 8 | Cooking Time: 18 Minutes

Ingredients:

- 1 egg
- 177ml milk
- ½ tsp baking soda
- ½ tsp espresso powder
- ½ tsp baking powder
- 50g cocoa powder
- 78ml vegetable oil
- 1 tsp apple cider vinegar
- 1 tsp vanilla
- 150g brown sugar
- 150g all-purpose flour
- ½ tsp salt

Directions:

1. In a bowl, whisk egg, vinegar, oil, brown sugar, vanilla, and milk.
2. Add flour, cocoa powder, baking soda, baking powder, espresso powder, and salt and stir until well combined.
3. Pour batter into the silicone muffin moulds.
4. Insert a crisper plate in Ninja Foodi air fryer baskets.
5. Place muffin moulds in both baskets.
6. Select zone 1 then select "bake" mode and set the temperature to 320 degrees F for 18 minutes. Press match cook to match zone 2 settings to zone 1. Press "start/stop" to begin.

Nutrition Info:

• (Per serving) Calories 222 | Fat 11g |Sodium 251mg | Carbs 29.6g | Fiber 2g | Sugar 14.5g | Protein 4g

Churros

Servings: 8 | Cooking Time: 10 Minutes

Ingredients:

- 1 cup water
- 1/3 cup unsalted butter, cut into cubes
- 2 tablespoons granulated sugar
- ¼ teaspoon salt
- 1 cup all-purpose flour
- 2 large eggs
- 1 teaspoon vanilla extract
- Cooking oil spray
- For the cinnamon-sugar coating:
- ½ cup granulated sugar
- ¾ teaspoon ground cinnamon

Directions:

1. Add the water, butter, sugar, and salt to a medium pot. Bring to a boil over medium-high heat.
2. Reduce the heat to medium-low and stir in the flour. Cook, stirring constantly with a rubber spatula until the dough is smooth and comes together.
3. Remove the dough from the heat and place it in a mixing bowl. Allow 4 minutes for cooling.
4. In a mixing bowl, beat the eggs and vanilla extract with an electric hand mixer or stand mixer until the dough comes together. The finished product will resemble gluey mashed potatoes. Press the lumps together into a ball with your hands, then transfer to a large piping bag with a large star-shaped tip. Pipe out the churros.
5. Install a crisper plate in both drawers. Place half the churros in the zone 1 drawer and half in zone 2's, then insert the drawers into the unit.
6. Select zone 1, select AIR FRY, set temperature to 390 degrees F/ 200 degrees C, and set time to 12 minutes. Select MATCH to match zone 2 settings to zone 1. Press the START/STOP button to begin cooking.
7. In a shallow bowl, combine the granulated sugar and cinnamon.
8. Immediately transfer the baked churros to the bowl with the sugar mixture and toss to coat.

Nutrition Info:

• (Per serving) Calories 204 | Fat 9g | Sodium 91mg | Carbs 27g | Fiber 0.3g | Sugar 15g | Protein 3g

Pumpkin Muffins With Cinnamon

Servings: 4 | Cooking Time: 20 Minutes

Ingredients:

- 1 and ½ cups all-purpose flour
- ½ teaspoon baking soda
- ½ teaspoon baking powder
- 1 and ¼ teaspoons cinnamon, groaned
- ¼ teaspoon ground nutmeg, grated
- 2 large eggs
- Salt, pinch
- ¾ cup granulated sugar
- ½ cup dark brown sugar
- 1 and ½ cups pumpkin puree
- ¼ cup coconut milk

Directions:

1. Take 4 ramekins and layer them with muffin paper.
2. In a bowl, add the eggs, brown sugar, baking soda, baking powder, cinnamon, nutmeg, and sugar and whisk well with an electric mixer.
3. In a second bowl, mix the flour, and salt.
4. Slowly add the dry ingredients to the wet ingredients.
5. Fold in the pumpkin puree and milk and mix it in well.
6. Divide this batter into 4 ramekins.
7. Place two ramekins in each air fryer basket.
8. Set the time for zone 1 to 18 minutes at 360 degrees F/ 180 degrees C on AIR FRY mode.
9. Select the MATCH button for the zone 2 basket.
10. Check after the time is up and if not done, and let it AIR FRY for one more minute.
11. Once it is done, serve.

Nutrition Info:

- (Per serving) Calories 291 | Fat 6.4g | Sodium 241mg | Carbs 57.1g | Fiber 4.4g | Sugar 42g | Protein 5.9g

Dehydrated Peaches

Servings: 4 | Cooking Time: 8 Hours

Ingredients:

- 300g canned peaches

Directions:

1. Insert a crisper plate in the Ninja Foodi air fryer baskets.
2. Place peaches in both baskets.
3. Select zone 1, then select "dehydrate" mode and set the temperature to 135 degrees F for 8 hours. Press "start/stop" to begin.

Nutrition Info:

- (Per serving) Calories 30 | Fat 0.2g |Sodium 0mg | Carbs 7g | Fiber 1.2g | Sugar 7g | Protein 0.7g

Mini Strawberry And Cream Pies

Servings:2 | Cooking Time:10

Ingredients:

- 1 box Store-Bought Pie Dough, Trader Joe's
- 1 cup strawberries, cubed
- 3 tablespoons of cream, heavy
- 2 tablespoons of almonds
- 1 egg white, for brushing

Directions:

1. Take the store brought pie dough and flatten it on a surface.
2. Use a round cutter to cut it into 3-inch circles.
3. Brush the dough with egg white all around the parameters.
4. Now add almonds, strawberries, and cream in a very little amount in the center of the dough, and top it with another circular.
5. Press the edges with the fork to seal it.
6. Make a slit in the middle of the dough and divide it into the baskets.
7. Set zone 1 to AIR FRY mode 360 degrees for 10 minutes.
8. Select MATCH for zone 2 basket.
9. Once done, serve.

Nutrition Info:

- (Per serving) Calories 203| Fat12.7g| Sodium 193mg | Carbs20 g | Fiber 2.2g | Sugar 5.8g | Protein 3.7g

Fried Dough With Roasted Strawberries

Servings:4 | Cooking Time: 20 Minutes

Ingredients:

- FOR THE FRIED DOUGH
- 6 ounces refrigerated pizza dough, at room temperature
- 2 tablespoons all-purpose flour, for dusting
- 4 tablespoons vegetable oil
- 2 tablespoons powdered sugar
- FOR THE ROASTED STRAWBERRIES
- 2 cups frozen whole strawberries
- 2 tablespoons granulated sugar

Directions:

1. To prep the fried dough: Divide the dough into four equal portions.
2. Dust a clean work surface with the flour. Place one dough portion on the surface and use a rolling pin to roll to a ⅛-inch thickness. Rub both sides of the dough with 1 tablespoon of oil. Repeat with remaining dough portions and oil.
3. To prep the strawberries: Place the strawberries in the Zone 2 basket. Sprinkle the granulated sugar on top.
4. To cook the fried dough and strawberries: Install a crisper plate in the Zone 1 basket. Place 2 dough portions in the basket and insert the basket in the unit. Insert the Zone 2 basket in the unit.
5. Select Zone 1, select AIR FRY, set the temperature to 400°F, and set the timer to 18 minutes.
6. Select Zone 2, select ROAST, set the temperature to 330°F, and set the timer to 20 minutes. Select SMART FINISH.
7. Press START/PAUSE to begin cooking.
8. When both timers read 8 minutes, press START/PAUSE. Remove the Zone 1 basket and transfer the fried dough to a cutting board. Place the 2 remaining dough portions in the basket, then reinsert the basket. Remove the Zone 2 basket and stir the strawberries. Reinsert the basket and press START/PAUSE to resume cooking.
9. When cooking is complete, the dough should be cooked through and the strawberries soft and jammy.
10. Sprinkle the fried dough with powdered sugar. Gently mash the strawberries with a fork. Spoon the strawberries onto each fried dough portion and serve.

Nutrition Info:

- (Per serving) Calories: 304; Total fat: 15g; Saturated fat: 2.5g; Carbohydrates: 38g; Fiber: 0.5g; Protein: 3g; Sodium: 421mg

Apple Hand Pies

Servings: 8 | Cooking Time: 21 Minutes.

Ingredients:

- 8 tablespoons butter, softened
- 12 tablespoons brown sugar
- 2 teaspoons cinnamon, ground
- 4 medium Granny Smith apples, diced
- 2 teaspoons cornstarch
- 4 teaspoons cold water
- 1 (14-oz) package pastry, 9-inch crust pie
- Cooking spray
- 1 tablespoon grapeseed oil
- ½ cup powdered sugar
- 2 teaspoons milk

Directions:

1. Toss apples with brown sugar, butter, and cinnamon in a suitable skillet.
2. Place the skillet over medium heat and stir cook for 5 minutes.
3. Mix cornstarch with cold water in a small bowl.
4. Add cornstarch mixture into the apple and cook for 1 minute until it thickens.
5. Remove this filling from the heat and allow it to cool.
6. Unroll the pie crust and spray on a floured surface.
7. Cut the dough into 16 equal rectangles.
8. Wet the edges of the 8 rectangles with water and divide the apple filling at the center of these rectangles.
9. Place the other 8 rectangles on top and crimp the edges with a fork, then make 2-3 slashes on top.
10. Place 4 small pies in each of the crisper plate.
11. Return the crisper plate to the Ninja Foodi Dual Zone Air Fryer.
12. Choose the Air Fry mode for Zone 1 and set the temperature to 390 degrees F and the time to 17 minutes.
13. Select the "MATCH" button to copy the settings for Zone 2.
14. Initiate cooking by pressing the START/STOP button.
15. Flip the pies once cooked halfway through, and resume cooking.
16. Meanwhile, mix sugar with milk.
17. Pour this mixture over the apple pies.
18. Serve fresh.

Nutrition Info:

- (Per serving) Calories 284 | Fat 16g |Sodium 252mg | Carbs 31.6g | Fiber 0.9g | Sugar 6.6g | Protein 3.7g

Mini Blueberry Pies

Servings:2 | Cooking Time:10

Ingredients:

- 1 box Store-Bought Pie Dough, Trader Joe's
- ¼ cup blueberry jam
- 1 teaspoon of lemon zest
- 1 egg white, for brushing

Directions:

1. Take the store brought pie dough and cut it into 3-inch circles.
2. Brush the dough with egg white all around the parameters.
3. Now add blueberry jam and zest in the middle and top it with another circular.
4. Press the edges with the fork to seal it.
5. Make a slit in the middle of the dough and divide it between the baskets.
6. Set zone 1 to AIR FRY mode 360 degrees for 10 minutes.
7. Select the MATCH button for zone 2.
8. Once cooked, serve.

Nutrition Info:

- (Per serving) Calories 234| Fat8.6g| Sodium187 mg | Carbs 38.2 g | Fiber 0.1g | Sugar13.7 g | Protein 2g

Victoria Sponge Cake

Servings: 8 | Cooking Time: 16 Minutes

Ingredients:

- Sponge Cake Ingredients
- 400g self-rising flour
- 450g caster sugar
- 50g lemon curd
- 200g butter
- 4 medium eggs
- 1 tablespoon vanilla essence
- 480ml skimmed milk
- 1 tablespoon olive oil
- 4 tablespoons strawberry jam
- Strawberry buttercream
- 115g butter
- 210g icing sugar
- ½ teaspoon strawberry food coloring
- 1 tablespoon single cream
- 1 teaspoon vanilla essence
- 1 teaspoon maple syrup

Directions:

1. Mix sugar and butter in a bowl using a hand mixer.
2. Beat eggs with oil, and vanilla in a bowl with the mixer until creamy.
3. Stir in milk, flour and curd then mix well.
4. Add butter mixture then mix well.
5. Divide this mixture in two 4 inches greased cake pans.
6. Place one pan in each air fryer basket.
7. Return the air fryer basket 1 to Zone 1, and basket 2 to Zone 2 of the Ninja Foodi 2-Basket Air Fryer.
8. Choose the "Air Fry" mode for Zone 1 and set the temperature to 375 degrees F and 16 minutes of cooking time.
9. Select the "MATCH COOK" option to copy the settings for Zone 2.
10. Initiate cooking by pressing the START/PAUSE BUTTON.
11. Meanwhile, blend the buttercream ingredients in a mixer until fluffy.
12. Place one cake on a plate and top it with the buttercream.
13. Top it jam and then with the other cake.
14. Serve.

Nutrition Info:

- (Per serving) Calories 284 | Fat 16g |Sodium 252mg | Carbs 31.6g | Fiber 0.9g | Sugar 6.6g | Protein 3.7g

Appendix : Recipes Index

"fried" Chicken With Warm Baked Potato Salad 38

A

Air Fried Lamb Chops 50
Air Fryer Sausage Patties 31
Air-fried Turkey Breast With Roasted Green Bean Casserole 44
Apple Crisp 81
Apple Crumble Peach Crumble 82
Apple Fritters 86
Apple Hand Pies 90
Asian Chicken 43
Avocado Fries With Sriracha Dip 18

B

Bacon And Egg Omelet 25
Bacon Wrapped Pork Tenderloin 52
Bagels 32
Baked Apples 87
Balsamic Duck Breast 35
Balsamic Steak Tips With Roasted Asparagus And Mushroom Medley 49
Balsamic Vegetables 69
Balsamic-glazed Tofu With Roasted Butternut Squash 78
Banana And Raisins Muffins 31
Barbecue Ribs With Roasted Green Beans And Shallots 48
Beef Jerky Pineapple Jerky 21
Beef Kofta Kebab 47
Beef Ribs Ii 51
Beets With Orange Gremolata And Goat's Cheese 76
Bell Peppers With Sausages 52
Biscuit Doughnuts 83
Blackened Mahimahi With Honey-roasted Carrots 67
Blueberry Coffee Cake And Maple Sausage Patties 26
Bread Pudding 83
Breakfast Bacon 29
Breakfast Cheese Sandwich 25
Breakfast Sausage Omelet 25
Breakfast Stuffed Peppers 33
Broccoli, Squash, & Pepper 71
Brussels Sprouts Potato Hash 24
Brussels Sprouts 79
Buffalo Bites 77
Buffalo Seitan With Crispy Zucchini Noodles 72

C

Caprese Panini With Zucchini Chips 74
Cauliflower Cheese Patties 17
Cheddar Quiche 21
Cheddar-stuffed Chicken 37
Cheese Corn Fritters 14
Cheesesteak Taquitos 47
Chicken And Broccoli 36
Chicken Breast Strips 37
Chicken Caprese 43
Chicken Drumsticks 38
Chicken Fajitas With Street Corn 45
Chicken Parmesan With Roasted Lemon-parmesan Broccoli 41
Chicken Parmesan 43
Chicken Potatoes 41
Chicken Stuffed Mushrooms 19
Chicken Tenders 22
Chicken Vegetable Skewers 39
Chicken Wings 39
Chili Chicken Wings 44
Chili Lime Tilapia 64
Chili-lime Crispy Chickpeas Pizza-seasoned Crispy Chickpeas 14
Chinese Bbq Pork 48
Chocolate Chip Cake 82
Chocolate Cookies 82
Churros 88
Cilantro Lime Steak 56
Cinnamon Sugar Dessert Fries 81
Cinnamon-raisin Bagels Everything Bagels 33
Cinnamon-sugar "churros" With Caramel Sauce 84
Cornbread 27
Cornish Hen With Asparagus 40
Crab Cake Poppers 19
Crispy Catfish 58
Crispy Fried Quail 35
Crispy Popcorn Shrimp 20
Crispy Tortilla Chips 15
Curry-crusted Lamb Chops With Baked Brown Sugar Acorn Squash 50

D

Dehydrated Peaches 89
Dijon Cheese Sandwich 17
Dijon Chicken Wings 42
Donuts 32
Dried Apple Chips Dried Banana Chips 15

E

Easy Breaded Pork Chops 54
Easy Pancake Doughnuts 29
Egg And Avocado In The Ninja Foodi 27
Egg White Muffins 28
Egg With Baby Spinach 30

F

Falafel 72
Fish And Chips 61
Fish Sandwich 61
Fresh Mix Veggies In Air Fryer 73
Fried Artichoke Hearts 70
Fried Dough With Roasted Strawberries 90
Fried Lobster Tails 65
Fried Olives 74
Fried Patty Pan Squash 79
Frozen Breaded Fish Fillet 64
Furikake Salmon 63

G

Garlic Bread 21
Garlic Butter Steaks 52
Garlic Potato Wedges In Air Fryer 70
Garlic-herb Fried Squash 75
Garlic-rosemary Brussels Sprouts 77
Green Salad With Crispy Fried Goat Cheese And Baked Croutons 69
Grill Cheese Sandwich 22

H

Hash Browns 32
Hasselback Potatoes 71
Healthy Lobster Cakes 59
Healthy Oatmeal Muffins 30
Healthy Semolina Pudding 84
Healthy Spinach Balls 16
Herb And Lemon Cauliflower 76
Herb Lemon Mussels 60
Herb Tuna Patties 59
Honey Banana Oatmeal 32
Honey Butter Chicken 37
Honey Lime Pineapple 81
Honey Teriyaki Tilapia 58

I

Italian Chicken & Potatoes 39

J

Jalapeño Popper Dip With Tortilla Chips 15
Jamaican Fried Chicken 42
Jelly Donuts 83
Jerk Tofu With Roasted Cabbage 73

K

Kale And Spinach Chips 77
Kale Potato Nuggets 17
Keto Baked Salmon With Pesto 66
Korean Bbq Beef 49

L

Lamb Shank With Mushroom Sauce 53
Lava Cake 87
Lemon Chicken Thighs 38
Lemon Pepper Fish Fillets 61
Lemon Pepper Salmon With Asparagus 65
Lemon Sugar Cookie Bars Monster Sugar Cookie Bars 84
Lemon-cream Cheese Danishes Cherry Danishes 29

M

Mac And Cheese Balls 20
Marinated Pork Chops 55
Mexican Jalapeno Poppers 20
Mini Blueberry Pies 91
Mini Strawberry And Cream Pies 89
Miso-glazed Shishito Peppers Charred Lemon Shishito Peppers 19
Moist Chocolate Espresso Muffins 88
Morning Egg Rolls 26

O

Oreo Rolls 86

P

Parmesan Crush Chicken 16
Parmesan Pork Chops 55
Pecan-crusted Catfish Nuggets With “fried” Okra 64
Pepper Egg Cups 31
Pepper Poppers 71
Pork Chops 50
Pork Tenderloin With Brown Sugar–pecan Sweet Potatoes 56
Potato And Parsnip Latkes With Baked Apples 75
Potato Chips 18
Potato Tater Tots 14
Potatoes & Beans 71
Pretzel-crusted Catfish 62
Pumpkin French Toast Casserole With Sweet And Spicy Twisted Bacon 28
Pumpkin Hand Pies Blueberry Hand Pies 87
Pumpkin Muffins With Cinnamon 89

R

Roasted Salmon And Parmesan Asparagus 62

S

Salmon With Coconut 62
Satay-style Tempeh With Corn Fritters 78
Saucy Carrots 76
Sausage Meatballs 54
Savory Salmon Fillets 66
Scallops 63
Sesame Honey Salmon 58
Short Ribs & Root Vegetables 55

Shrimp Po'boys With Sweet Potato Fries 60
Shrimp Skewers 64
Smoked Salmon 63
Spicy Chicken Tenders 17
Spicy Chicken Wings 40
Spicy Lamb Chops 52
Steak And Mashed Creamy Potatoes 47
Steak Bites With Cowboy Butter 53
Steak In Air Fry 48
Strawberry Baked Oats Chocolate Peanut Butter Baked Oats 24
Stuffed Bell Peppers 22
Stuffed Tomatoes 77
Sweet Potato Hash 31
Sweet Potato Sausage Hash 27

T

Tasty Lamb Patties 51
Tasty Parmesan Shrimp 66
Tasty Sweet Potato Wedges 18
Teriyaki Chicken Skewers 40
Thai Chicken Meatballs 36
Thai Curry Chicken Kabobs 45
Tofu Veggie Meatballs 21
Tomahawk Steak 51
Tuna Patties 66
Tuna Steaks 59
Turkey Burger Patties 37

V

Victoria Sponge Cake 91

W

Walnuts Fritters 85

Y

Yellow Potatoes With Eggs 30

Z

Zesty Cranberry Scones 85
Zucchini Cakes 70
Zucchini Pork Skewers 54

Printed in Great Britain
by Amazon

23454999R00057